The
BEADER'S
Bible

The BEADER'S Bible

Over 300 great charts for beadweavers

Claire Crouchley

krause

A Quarto Book

First published in North America in 2004
by Krause Publications, 700 East State Street
Iola, WI 54990–0001

Library of Congress Catalog Card No
2004093867

ISBN 0 87349 905 0

QUAR.BDB

Conceived, designed, and produced by
Quarto Publishing plc
The Old Brewery, 6 Blundell Street,
London N7 9BH

Senior project editor Gillian Haslam
Art editor Claire Van Rhyn
Designer Penny Dawes
Assistant art director Penny Cobb
Photographer Colin Bowling, Paul Forrester
Indexer Pamela Ellis

Art director Moira Clinch
Publisher Piers Spence

Manufactured in Singapore by Universal
Graphics Pte Ltd
Printed in China by Midas Printing
International Ltd

For my mum,
without whom this
book would *never*
have been finished.

Contents

Introduction

Beadweaving has a long history, stretching over thousands of years and across all continents. It has soared in popularity in recent years as people discover the beauty and versatility of this traditional craft.

New techniques in glass production have resulted in an amazing range of colors and styles of beads, allowing anyone to produce wonderfully embellished items. I defy any craft-lover to walk into a bead store and not be inspired by the selection of beads offered.

One of the great appeals of beadwork is that you need so few tools. With just a needle, thread, scissors, and some tiny beads, you're on your way to producing beautiful pieces! In the tools and materials section of this book you'll find a summary of these and a few other useful (although not essential) items to guide you on your way to beginning weaving.

The techniques section acts as an introduction to some classic off-loom beadweaving stitches, as well as providing instructions on how to use a loom.

The main focus of this book is the pattern directory where you'll find more than 300 patterns on a wide range of subjects. These are all in a standard range of sizes, which means you can mix and match. Why not make a bracelet decorated with moons and stars, or an amulet bag with your initial and a border of daisies? Play with the colors, and let your imagination take over.

And while you're playing, why not go out and meet a few like-minded people? Beading groups meet up all over the world, where people get together to covet each other's bead stash, admire one another's work, and offer helpful hints and tips. If you can't find a group near you, make beading buddies through one of the many groups on the internet. You'll find a few starting points in the address section at the back of this book. Have fun.

How to use this book

All the materials and basic techniques are described in the front section of the book. The beading patterns are organized into eleven themed chapters within the pattern directory.

Stitch symbol I
Two stitch symbols are used in the directory. This squared-up symbol shows the sample has been beaded either using square stitch (see page 30) or on a loom (see page 34). Both methods give the same finished result.

Stitch symbol 2
This zigzag symbol shows the sample has been beaded using either peyote stitch (see page 23) or brick stitch (see page 27). Both stitches give the same finished result.

Photograph
This shows the finished beaded pattern. A note tells you whether it's reproduced actual size.

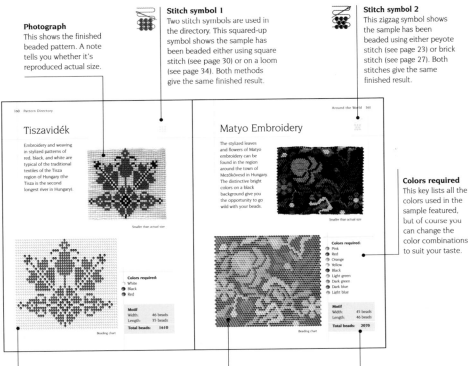

Colors required
This key lists all the colors used in the sample featured, but of course you can change the color combinations to suit your taste.

Starting point
The direction of beading for each design depends on which stitch is used (see pages 23–37 in the techniques section). For all stitches, the first bead to be picked up is the one in the bottom left corner of the pattern unless there is an arrow indicating the book should be turned sideways. If using peyote stitch, read the pattern upward. For all other stitches, read along the bottom row toward the right.

Chart
A full-color chart is provided for each design, showing the color sequence for threading the beads.

Beads required
This panel lists the total number of beads required for the design, which is an indicator of how long a design is going to take and how costly it will be to make.

BEADING
BASICS

TOOLS AND MATERIALS

One of the great things about the craft of beading is that you need very few tools and supplies to get you started—just a selection of beads, a needle, some thread, scissors, and a surface to work on.

Beads

It's very easy to become addicted to beads as they are available in such a fantastic range of colors and finishes. This section explains which beads are suitable for which projects.

Seed beads

These are the beads used for all the patterns in this book, and are also known as rocailles. You will usually find seed beads come from Japan or the Czech Republic, although there are several other countries that produce them. The Japanese beads tend to be slightly larger, are closer to a square in shape, and have a larger hole. Czech beads are smaller, slightly flattened so they are more oval in shape, and have a smaller hole. Try using both and see which style of bead you prefer to work with, but bear in mind that because of the difference in size and shape, it is better to work with one or the other within one piece of beadwork.

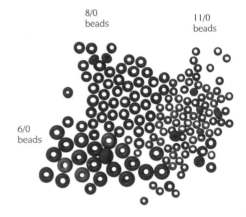

6/0 beads

8/0 beads

11/0 beads

Sizing Seed beads come in a variety of sizes, with the most common being 6/0, 8/0, 11/0 and 15/0 (the larger the number, the smaller the bead). This naming system arose because at one time the smallest available size of bead was 0. When a smaller size was produced this was labeled 00, the next smallest was 000, and so on. Eventually the quantity of zeros became too cumbersome to use easily, so the system was changed and a number was used to show how many zeros there were. Thus 000000 became 6/0. You might also see this written as 6^0.

Czech beads

Japanese beads

Although this sizing system is commonly used, a size 11/0 bead from one manufacturer may be a slightly different size to an 11/0 bead from another manufacturer. Using beads of different sizes within one piece can cause the beadwork to buckle slightly. For some items this may not matter, but if you prefer a smooth piece of bead "fabric," try to use only beads from one manufacturer within a piece of beadwork.

The most commonly used size is 11/0, and all the examples in this book were made with this size. However, other sizes of seed beads can be used to make any of the patterns featured in this book, and the only difference will be the finished size.

Colors Made from glass, seed beads come in a stunning range of colors,

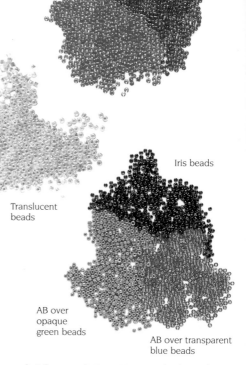

Transparent red-lined and blue purple-lined beads

Satin beads

Translucent beads

Iris beads

AB over opaque green beads

AB over transparent blue beads

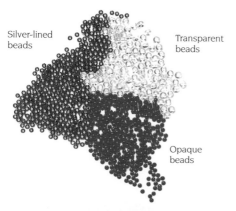

Silver-lined beads

Transparent beads

Opaque beads

finishes, and sizes. You can find a color to suit every design, and they are more than a little addictive!

The beads themselves can be:

Transparent—made of clear glass so you can see right through the bead.

Translucent—the glass is slightly milky, so light can still pass through it. Also sometimes called opal.

Opaque—the glass is a solid color, and light cannot pass through it.

Silver-lined—the hole at the center of the bead has a mirror-like lining, making the bead sparkle. Although silver or silver gilt are the most commonly used metals, you can also buy copper, bronze, and even gold-lined beads.

Ceylon beads

Color-lined—the hole through the center of the bead is lined with a different color. Sometimes this is a separate layer of glass, but it can also be a fine layer of paint applied to the inside of the bead. Translucent beads lined with white are known as white-hearts, and this effect can intensify the color of the bead.

Pearl beads

Luster beads

Satin—the glass is striated, and this gives an effect like the mineral tiger-eye, or satin fabric.

Finishes As well as color, there can also be a finish applied to the surface of the bead, such as:

AB—Aurora borealis. A clear rainbow finish over the bead.

Iris—an iridescent finish applied to an opaque bead, giving it a metallic look.

Luster—a shiny finish. This can be clear, colored, or metallic—for example, gold luster beads which have a lovely warm glow. An opaque lustered bead is called "pearl" and a translucent lustered bead is called "ceylon."

Matte—the glass is etched, giving a soft, frosted finish.

Metallic/galvanized—a metal finish or coating applied to the bead. Although some of these can last well, this finish can wear off with handling.

Painted/dyed—some beads are painted or dyed in order to obtain colors that are difficult to produce in glass, such as strong pinks and purples. Although these beads are beautiful, the paint can wear off when the beads are handled or fade in sunlight, so if you use these colors, take care of the finished piece.

If you are worried about a finish or color on a bead, try asking the supplier for more information. Many bead stores will be able to tell you whether a color is likely to rub off or not.

More finishes are coming on to the market all the time. To make the choice even wider, finishes can be combined, so there are matte, silver-lined beads, or transparent, matte, AB beads. Don't let this worry you—just enjoy your beads and choose the perfect colors for your project.

Matte beads

Metallic/galvanized beads

Cylinder beads

Also suitable for use with the patterns in this book, these beads are made in Japan under the trade names Delica and Treasure. They are very precisely cut cylinders, with a large hole through the center of the bead, and come in a wide range of colors and finishes. The larger hole makes them easier to work with as the needle is able to pass through the bead a number of times with ease. The beads fit together perfectly when woven, and, because of the regular size and cylinder shape, they produce a smooth bead "fabric" a little stiffer than when seed beads are used. However, this enhanced quality is reflected in the price.

For some projects, the finish is worth the price of the cylinder beads, but at other times the slightly rougher finish of seed beads is preferable. If you can, try them both to see which you prefer.

Cylinder beads

Embellishment beads

When you've finished your weaving, you may want to decorate it with some extra beads, and the range of beautiful beads available is very tempting.

Some of the more well-known types of bead are bugles (long, thin, cylinder-shaped beads), cubes, triangles, daggers, and Magatamas (teardrop).

Three types of bugle beads

Close-up of cylinder beads

Cubes and
triangles

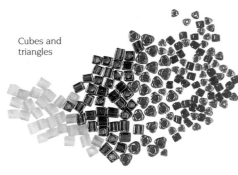

Dagger
beads

A quick browse through a bead store,
catalog, or website will also reveal
beads in the shape of leaves, flowers,
faces, fish, bicones, crystals, stars…
The list goes on and on, and all of
these beads are beautiful.

Magatamas
(teardrop
beads)

However, do take care when using
bugles. These beads sometimes have
sharp edges and can cut your thread.
Check the beads before you use them,
and when stringing several bugles in
a row, put a seed bead inbetween
them as a buffer.

If you're feeling really
adventurous, try buying
some lampwork glass
beads to add to your
beadwork. These
range from mass-
produced beads
from India, to
one-of-a-kind
beads made by
artists all over the
world. Lampwork glass beads can
add a special finishing touch to a
piece of beadwork.

A variety
of shapes

Crystal
beads

Thread

There are a variety of threads on the market for beadweaving, many of them made from a form of nylon. Two of the most popular were originally developed for upholstery, and are flexible, fine, and strong.

Nymo is made of nylon monofilaments and comes in a range of sizes. Size D is suitable for most beadwork with size 11/0 seed beads or Delicas, but you may wish to use size B for work where you pass the needle through each bead several times, as in square stitch. Nymo can be bought on bobbins in a variety of colors, or on spools and cones in black or white. The thread on a spool or cone is a little thicker and harder wearing than on a bobbin, but both varieties work well.

Silamide is a twisted nylon thread, with a size roughly equivalent to size A or B in Nymo. This is usually available on a card or in spools, and comes in a great range of colors. It is a little harder to thread, and as it is finer some people prefer to use it doubled.

Fishing lines sold under the brand names PowerPro, SpiderLine, and Fire Line are all made from Dynema, a gel-spun polyethylene. They are strong, flexible, and the 10lb test weight and below should be fine enough to use for bead-weaving. These are relatively new to the market and are gaining in popularity. Be careful when buying fishing line, as other brands can be deliberately designed to degrade over time.

Cotton or silk threads are also occasionally used. However, this is not recommended as although they can be strong when first used, they have a tendency to fray and break in time.

Choosing a color

The thread needs to blend into the beadwork as much as possible, so choose a color that matches the main colors of bead used. Don't forget that the thread will show on transparent and translucent beads (blue thread used with blue transparent beads will make the color deeper, while yellow thread will make the beads appear a little green). If you use white thread, you can always color any thread that shows with a marker pen, and some people feel that black thread makes the colors appear brighter.

A selection of the various threads used in beading. Experiment with different types to discover which you find easiest to work with.

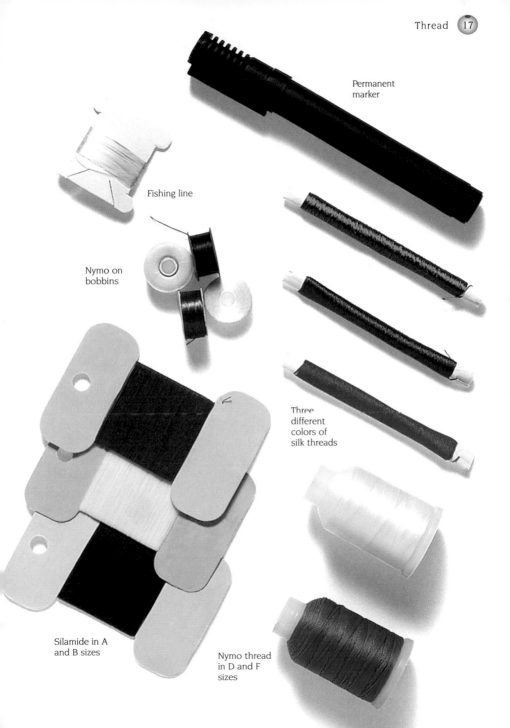

Permanent marker

Fishing line

Nymo on bobbins

Three different colors of silk threads

Silamide in A and B sizes

Nymo thread in D and F sizes

Basic Kit

You need very few tools to begin beading—needles and a pair of scissors are the only essentials—but a few extras can help.

Beading needles are available in a variety of sizes—the larger the number, the smaller the diameter of the needle. Sizes 10 to 13 are ideal to use with size 11/0 seed beads. Some beaders like to coat their thread with a fine layer of beeswax to reduce knotting and fraying.

A sharp pair of scissors is essential. Buy a good pair, and don't use them for cutting paper!

A small pair of pliers can be useful when attaching jewelry findings. They can also be used to gain a grip on the needle if you have difficulty pulling it through the bead, but be careful not to pull too hard or you risk breaking the bead.

If you want to attach your beadwork to something like a greetings card or picture frame, then strong glue may be useful (see the Finishing Off section at the end of the book).

If you do tie any knots, a drop of clear nail varnish will seal them.

A good light source will be useful. If possible, sit near a window if you are beading during the day, and have a good lamp available to shine on your work as it becomes dark. Most artificial lights have an orange tint that will alter the shade of your beads. If this is a problem for you, using a daylight bulb that has a blue tint closer to natural light may help.

Beading tools are all quite small and portable.

Pliers with cutting edge

Clippers

Scissors

Thread conditioner in holder

Needles in various sizes

Beeswax

Glue

Clear nail varnish

Work Surface and Storage

Choosing the right surface for beading will make it easier for you. There are several options, so try them all to find the one that suits you best.

Every beader has their own favorite surface to bead on. These include plastic or china painting palettes, which have separate compartments to sort beads into, and trays, bowls, and boxes. Any of these can be lined with leather, suede, or velvet, which give a smooth surface so the beads won't bounce away. If you plan to work when traveling, it is useful to carry a piece of suedette (imitation suede), to spread out on any convenient flat surface. Make sure your surface is a plain color, either light or dark, so that you can see the beads clearly against it

There is a wide variety of options for storing beads. Plastic bags are easy to store, and you can see the colors of the beads easily, but they do tend to split. You can buy boxes with separate compartments to sort beads into. These are easy to transport, but it can be difficult to get beads out of the compartments, and small beads may jump between compartments when the lid is closed. A piece of foam placed across the top of the box, beneath the lid, can reduce this. Small containers such as film canisters, paperclip boxes, or jars may also be useful.

A toolbox is good for transporting your beads and equipment, and a small

Store beads neatly so sizes, shapes, and colors do not become mixed up, and keep a beading surface with them.

chest with a variety of drawers helps you keep things neat at home. There are also several specially designed bead storage systems on the market, so have a look in catalogs and on websites.

Looms

A wide variety of looms is available, from reasonably priced ones ideal for the beginner, to extremely expensive models.

Many commercially available looms are designed to make long, thin pieces of beadwork, but if you wish to make a wider piece, simply make it in two halves, and then join these together (see page 37).

If you're just starting beadwork and want to try weaving on a loom without spending a lot of money, then a small wire loom is probably the best model to choose.

If you'd like to use something a little sturdier than the wire loom, there is a variety of wooden frame looms available.

Finally, for something a little different try the bracelet loom or tube loom. This is only suitable for small pieces, but is very inexpensive.

The best advice really is to look on websites, browse through catalogs, and visit bead and craft stores to see what is available. Do ask other beaders for their recommendations as well.

Left: a wooden loom
Below: a wire loom

Materials for Finishing

Once you've finished weaving your piece of beadwork, you'll want to turn it into something useful and/or decorative.

Findings are the metal components used to turn your beading into unique items of jewelry. The findings can be made of anything from cheap base metals to one-of-a-kind silver and gold creations. Examples include clasps for bracelets and necklaces, earwires for clip-on or pierced earrings, brooch backs, barrette backs, and keyrings.

You can mount your work onto blank greetings cards—these, along with a range of attractive papers for decoration, can be found in craft stores and stationery suppliers.

Keep your eyes open in craft and hardware stores for materials to finish your beadwork.

To keep your work on display, you may wish to frame it. Check your local craft store for papers and accessories to mount and frame it. It's also worth a look at the range of wrapping papers available to use as backing paper.

Items such as curtain rings can be found at hardware stores, to create items for your home.

Small pieces of imitation suede such as suedette or ultrasuede are useful for backing beadwork. Some bead stores stock these, or try suppliers of fabrics for making teddy bears.

Curtain rings

Paper, cardboard. and suedette for backing bead pieces

Jewelry findings

Frames

TECHNIQUES

On the following pages you'll find instructions for four different techniques that will each produce a "fabric" of beads. The three stitches are peyote, brick, and square stitch, and the techniques of loom weaving are also covered.

Peyote Stitch

This is a stitch with a long history, and it is still very popular today. It produces a flexible fabric of beads in a brick-like pattern of staggered rows. This is a good stitch for weaving a long strip, such as a bracelet.

All the beads in the following diagrams are shown widely spaced with the thread clearly visible. This is so that the diagrams are easier to follow. When you are weaving, the beads should be close together so that no thread is showing.

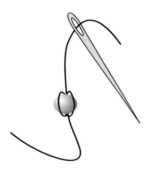

1 Start with approximately 2 yards (2m) of thread. String a bead onto the thread, about 6in (15cm) from the end, and then loop through it again twice. This is the stop bead, and it will prevent the other beads from falling off the thread.

2 Pick up the beads for the first two rows and the first bead of the third row. Slide these down the thread as far as the stop bead. Pass the needle through the third bead from the needle (blue), heading back toward the stop bead.

3 Pick up the next bead of the third row, and pass through the second bead from the needle (blue), still working toward the stop bead. Repeat until the end of the row. The beads should now have a staggered edge, with "up" beads (red) and "down" beads (blue). Don't worry if the strip of beads is twisted at this point as it will straighten out over the next few rows.

4 To start the fourth row, pick up the first bead and reverse the direction, so you are now working away from the stop bead. Pass through the first "up" bead. Continue along the row, picking up a bead and passing through the next "up" bead until you reach the end of the row.

5 Continue weaving, reversing the direction at the end of each row so that you work up and down the piece. Each time, pick up the next bead and pass through the next "up" bead, until you reach the end of the pattern, or run out of thread.

A woven sample of peyote stitch, showing the interlocking rows of beads.

Fastening off thread

The best way to fasten off the ends of
thread is to weave them into the
beadwork. This is secure, and doesn't
show as there aren't any knots.

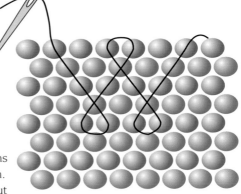

Fasten off when there is about
6in (15cm) thread remaining.
Weave the thread into the
beadwork, changing direction several times.
This means the thread is securely anchored
as any tension on the threads simply tightens
the loops made when you reversed direction.
It is best to change direction three times. Cut
the thread off close to the beadwork.

Start a new piece of thread by weaving it into the beads in
the same way to anchor the end.

At this point you can also fasten off the start of the thread
by removing the stop bead and weaving the thread into your
work in this way.

Reading the pattern

In peyote stitch the rows are counted
on the diagonal.

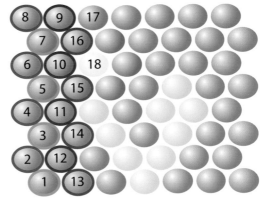

Here the first row is outlined in red,
the second in green, the third in blue,
and the fourth row in purple. The beads
are numbered in the order that they are
picked up.

When stitching the patterns in this
book with peyote stitch, always begin in
the bottom left-hand corner, and work
your way toward the top, picking up the
first two rows. Then begin on row three
working down the pattern (steps 2 and 3 in the earlier
instructions). Continue until you reach the end of the pattern.

Joining peyote stitch

You may sometimes wish to link the two ends of a piece of peyote to make a tube. Do this before weaving in the thread ends. This method can also be used to join two different pieces of peyote stitch together. You can join the straight sides of a piece of peyote stitch using the same method as for brick stitch (see page 29).

Make sure that you have woven an even number of rows of peyote. A quick way to check this is to compare the two ends of the piece—they should fit together.

Bend the piece of beadwork into a tube, and match the two ends together. Where there is an "up" bead on one side, there should be a "down" bead on the other side, and vice versa. If you have an odd number of rows, there will be "up" or "down" beads in the same position on each side so you will need either to work one more row, or unpick one row.

Your thread should be currently coming out of a "down" bead at the end of one side of the beadwork. Pass the needle through the "up" bead on the opposite side of the piece of beadwork. Go back to the first side of beadwork, and pass the needle through the next "up" bead. Continue in this way, picking up the next "up" bead on the opposite side with each stitch, until you reach the end. As you pull the thread tight you will see the beads lock together, with each "up" bead slotting between two "up" beads on the other side.

Once you reach the top, pass down through the "down" bead opposite to the one the thread is coming out of in order to link the two ends completely. Weave in the ends of thread in the usual way to finish.

Brick Stitch

Also known as Comanche stitch, this produces a brick-like pattern of staggered rows, slightly more flexible than peyote. Once woven it's very difficult to tell them apart, but the technique is totally different.

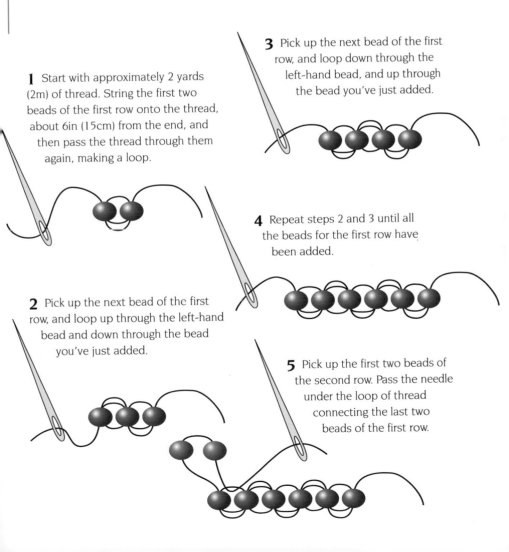

3 Pick up the next bead of the first row, and loop down through the left-hand bead, and up through the bead you've just added.

1 Start with approximately 2 yards (2m) of thread. String the first two beads of the first row onto the thread, about 6in (15cm) from the end, and then pass the thread through them again, making a loop.

4 Repeat steps 2 and 3 until all the beads for the first row have been added.

2 Pick up the next bead of the first row, and loop up through the left-hand bead and down through the bead you've just added.

5 Pick up the first two beads of the second row. Pass the needle under the loop of thread connecting the last two beads of the first row.

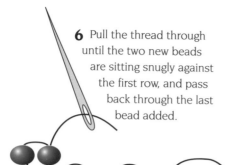

6 Pull the thread through until the two new beads are sitting snugly against the first row, and pass back through the last bead added.

8 Start the next row in the same way, but working back in the other direction. Carry on adding rows until you reach the end of the pattern.

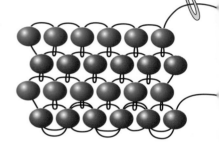

7 Pick up the next bead of the second row. Pass the needle under the next loop of thread, and back up through the bead you just added. Continue in this way until you reach the end of the row.

Weave in the thread ends and start new threads in the same way as for peyote stitch (see page 25).

A woven sample of brick stitch. Notice how similar its appearance is to peyote stitch.

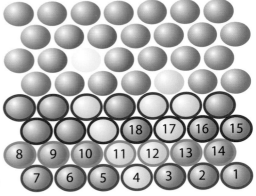

Reading the pattern

In brick stitch rows are counted horizontally starting from the bottom. Here, the first row is outlined in red, the second in green, the third in blue, and the fourth row in purple. The beads are numbered in the order that they are picked up.

When stitching the patterns in this book with brick stitch, always begin in the bottom right-hand corner, and work your way along the first row to the left. Then begin on row two working to the right. Reverse the direction with each row so that you work back and forth along the pattern, climbing upward. Continue until you reach the end of the pattern.

Joining brick stitch

If you wish to link the two ends of a piece of brick stitch to make a tube, do this before weaving in the thread ends. You can use this method to join two different pieces of brick stitch together, as well as to make a tube, and can join the staggered sides of a piece of brick stitch using the same method as for peyote stitch (see page 26).

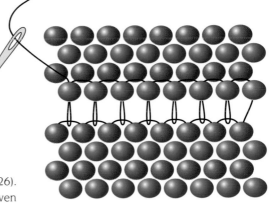

Make sure that you have woven an even number of rows.

Joining is done in the same way as adding a new row, but this time each new bead you pick up is already part the first row you stitched.

Once you reach the end, weave in the ends of thread in the usual way (see page 25).

Square Stitch

Sometimes called faux loom stitch, as the beads are organized in neat columns and rows in the same way as loom weaving, this produces a strong fabric that is fairly stiff with rows and columns of beads.

1 Start with approximately 2 yards (2m) of thread. String a bead onto the thread, about 6in (15cm) from the end, and then loop through it again twice. This is the stop bead, and it will prevent the other beads from falling off the thread as they are picked up.

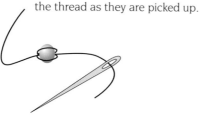

2 Pick up all the beads for the first row, and the first bead of the second row, and slide these down the thread to join the stop bead. Loop through the last two beads added, and pull the thread tight. Don't worry if the beads are not lying next to each other as in the diagram—when the rest of the second row is added, these should straighten out.

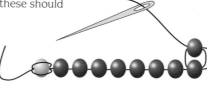

3 Pick up the second bead of the second row. Pass through the second bead from the right on the first row, taking the thread through the bead from left to right.

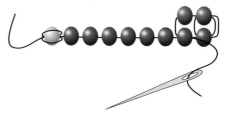

4 Pass back though the bead that you've just added from right to left.

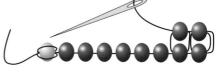

5 As each bead is added, it sits directly above one of the beads from the row below. Continue adding beads to the second row, following the pattern from right to left, by picking up the next bead in the row and looping through the bead below it in the first row and back through the bead you've just added.

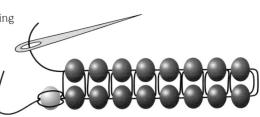

6 Begin the next row in the same way, but working in the opposite direction. So this time, pick up the first bead of the next row, pass through the bead below it from right to left, and back through the new bead from left to right.

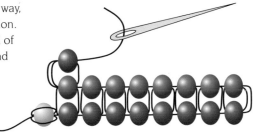

7 Continue adding rows until you reach the end of the pattern.

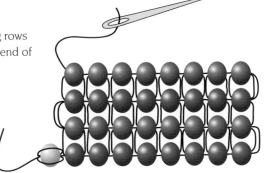

A woven sample
of square stitch,
with the beads
neatly lined up
in rows.

Starting and ending thread

The best way to fasten off the ends of thread is to weave them
into the beadwork. This is secure, and as there are no knots it
doesn't show.

Fasten off when there is about 6in (15cm) thread remaining.
Weave the thread into the beadwork, changing direction several
times. This way the thread is securely anchored as any tension
on the threads simply tightens the loops made when you
reversed direction. It is best to change
direction three times,
and then cut the thread
off close to the beadwork.

Start a new piece of thread
by weaving it into the beads in
the same way to anchor the end.

At this point you can also fasten
off the start of the thread, by
removing the stop bead and weaving
the thread into your work in this way.

Reading the pattern

In square stitch rows are counted horizontally starting from the bottom.

Here the first row is outlined in red, the second in green, the third in blue, and the fourth row in purple. The beads are numbered in the order they are picked up.

When stitching the patterns in this book with square stitch, always begin in one of the bottom corners, and work your way along the first row. Then begin the second row working in the opposite direction. Reverse the direction with each row so that you work back and forth along the pattern, climbing upward. Continue until you reach the end of the pattern.

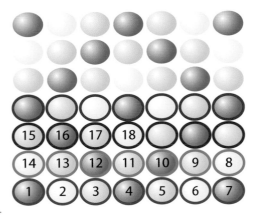

Joining the ends

You may sometimes wish to link the two ends of a piece of square stitch to make a tube. Do this before weaving in the thread ends.

This is done in the same way as adding a new row, but this time each new bead you pick up is already part the first row you stitched.

Once you reach the end, weave in the ends of thread in the normal way.

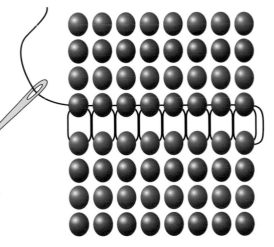

Loom Weaving

Once you've started, this is the fastest way to bead, but it does take a while to set the loom up and to weave in all the ends of thread. This produces the softest, most flexible "fabric" of the four stitches.

When weaving on the loom you will have to learn a few new terms. The warp is the thread wound onto your loom. To warp the loom is when you put the warp thread onto the loom. The weft thread is the thread with beads on that is woven onto the warp.

Warping the loom

1 All looms are different, so while this is a basic method for warping, check the instructions that come with your loom. You will need one more warp thread than the number of beads across the pattern. For example, for a pattern eight beads wide, you will need nine warp threads.

To decide how long the warp will be, use the length of your project plus 12in (30cm) to fasten off with (6in/15cm for each end) plus twice the length of the fringe (if you are going to add one).

a) If your loom has rollers, and you will be making a piece longer than the loom, you need to cut a length of thread for each warp. Tie the warp thread to one roller, and wind this up until you have just enough of the warp threads left to reach the other roller. Line the threads up in the coils at the top and bottom of the loom, and tie to the bottom roller. As you weave, use the rollers to wind your work on.

b) If your loom doesn't have rollers, or you are making a piece that will fit on the loom, tie one end of your spool of thread to one end of the loom. Take the warp thread through the coils at the top and bottom of the loom, lining it up, and wrap around the nail or screw at the bottom of the loom. Go back through the coils at the bottom and top of the loom, right next to your first thread. Continue until you have enough warp threads, and tie the end of the thread off.

2 Start with roughly 2 yards (2m) of thread, and tie one end to one of the outside warp threads with an overhand knot. Leave a 6in (15cm) tail so you can fasten the end in later.

3 Pick up all the beads for the first row, slide the beads to the end of the thread, and pass the weft thread under all the warp threads. Pull the weft thread taut.

4 Use your index finger to push the beads up between the weft-threads, and pass the needle back through all the beads, keeping the needle above the warp threads. It is important to make sure that the needle is above the warp threads, or the beads will not be secured properly.

5 Continue adding rows in this way until you reach the end of the pattern.

6 When you are near the end of a piece of thread, leave at least 6in (15cm) hanging after you finish adding a row. Start a new piece of thread as before, leaving a 6in (15cm) tail hanging, and continue weaving. These ends can be woven into the piece later (see page 36).

Fastening off

Once you have finished the pattern weave in the thread ends in the same way as for square stitch (see page 32). Take your work off the loom. All those warp threads now have to be secured and there are a few different ways to take care of these threads.

Leave a fringe This is the easiest and quickest way to finish your work. Simply tie the threads together in groups of three or four with an overhand knot, and then trim them to the same length. If you slip a needle into the center of the knot before you tighten it, you can use the needle to position the knot next to the beadwork. If you wish to add a beaded fringe, see the section on Finishing Off (page 245).

Selvedge ends Do this before taking your work off the loom. This method is useful if the back of the work won't show, for example on a brooch or a picture. Once you've finished weaving the pattern, weave a selvedge edge using only the weft thread with no beads on it, taking the thread under and over the warp threads.

Continue in this way until you've woven at least ¼in (5mm). Do the same at the other end of your beadwork. Take the work off the loom, knot the warp threads in pairs (knot the end of the weft

thread with one pair), and trim them. Fold the selvedge edges under the beadwork and glue them down.

Weaving in the ends This takes time and patience, but make a cup of coffee, put some music on, and you'll soon find that you've finished it. Weave each warp thread into the beadwork in the same way as for square stitch (see page 32). Take threads down varying numbers of rows, so that you don't fill the beads at the end of your piece with thread.

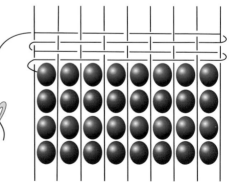

Reading the pattern

Loom weaving creates a pattern with columns of beads. Rows are counted up from the bottom. Here the first row is outlined in red, the second in green, the third in blue, and the fourth in purple. The beads are numbered in the order they are picked up.

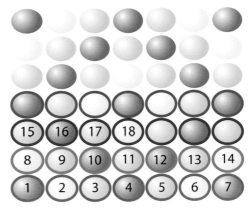

When weaving the patterns in this book on a loom, always begin in one of the bottom corners, and work your way along the first row. Then start on row two from the same side. So if you start in the bottom left-hand corner, read each row from left to right. You will need to turn the book sideways to follow the charts for a few of the border patterns, but this is clearly marked on the pages.

Joining the ends

Once the warp threads have been woven in, loom work can be made into a tube following the instructions for square stitch to attach the top row to the bottom row (see page 33).

To attach the side rows to each other, follow the diagram above, weaving the thread from side to side.

If you want to make a piece that is wider than your loom, weave it as several separate pieces and join them together this way.

PATTERN
DIRECTORY

PATTERN
SELECTOR

This section presents all the patterns
featured in this book. This will enable you
to see what is available at a glance, and
to mix and match borders to surround
your main design. Remember that you can
easily change the shades of the beads if
you like the design but wish to make it in
an alternative colorway. The page numbers
are given below the designs.

Geometrics

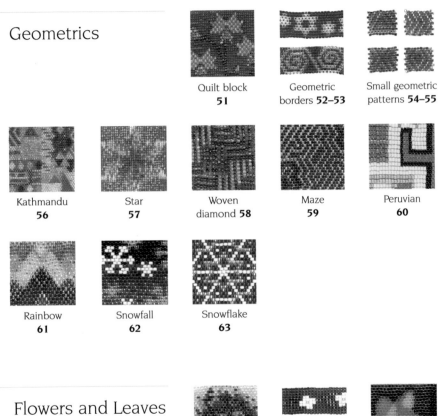

Quilt block
51

Geometric
borders **52–53**

Small geometric
patterns **54–55**

Kathmandu
56

Star
57

Woven
diamond **58**

Maze
59

Peruvian
60

Rainbow
61

Snowfall
62

Snowflake
63

Flowers and Leaves

Flower basket
65

Floral borders
66–69

Daffodil
70

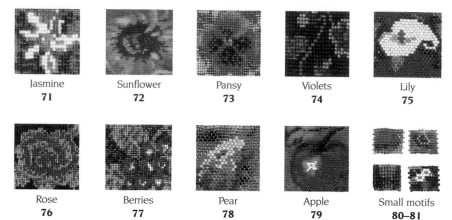

Jasmine **71**	Sunflower **72**	Pansy **73**	Violets **74**	Lily **75**
Rose **76**	Berries **77**	Pear **78**	Apple **79**	Small motifs **80–81**

Fur and Feathers

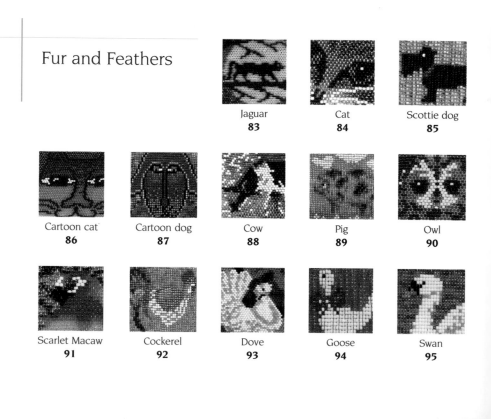

Jaguar **83**	Cat **84**	Scottie dog **85**

Cartoon cat **86**	Cartoon dog **87**	Cow **88**	Pig **89**	Owl **90**
Scarlet Macaw **91**	Cockerel **92**	Dove **93**	Goose **94**	Swan **95**

Indian elephant	Zebra	Animal borders
96	**97**	**98–101**

Marine

Marine borders	Clown fish	Starfish
103	**104**	**105**

Seahorse	Dolphin	Seashell	Small marine	Lighthouse
106	**107**	**108**	motifs **109**	**110**

Boat
110

Seasons

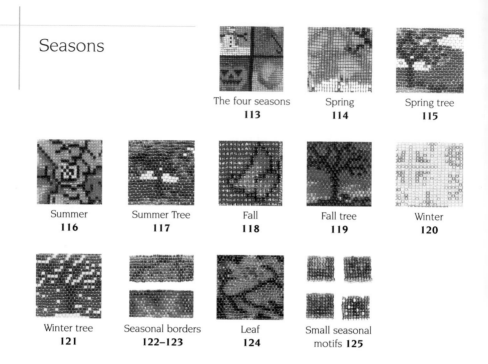

The four seasons
113

Spring
114

Spring tree
115

Summer
116

Summer Tree
117

Fall
118

Fall tree
119

Winter
120

Winter tree
121

Seasonal borders
122–123

Leaf
124

Small seasonal
motifs **125**

Celestial Bodies

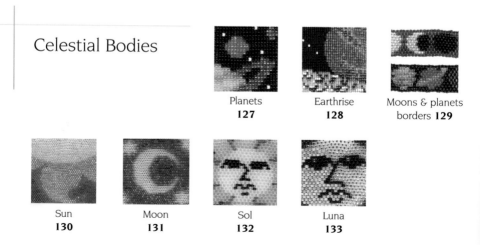

Planets
127

Earthrise
128

Moons & planets
borders **129**

Sun
130

Moon
131

Sol
132

Luna
133

Around the World

Celtic knot
135

Celtic bird
136

Celtic spiral
137

Celtic borders
138

Green man
139

Japanese Crane
140

Geisha
141

Japanese tiles
142

Japanese pine
143

Chinese dragon
144

Ginger jar
145

Nepalese eyes
146

Eye of Horus
147

Scarab
148

African drummer
149

African pattern
150

African borders
151

Ontovalo sun
152

Indian scrollwork
pattern **153**

Indian dancer
154

Las Chismosas
155

Native American
borders **156–157**

Russian domes
158

Cornflower
159

Tiszavidék
160

Matyo embroidery
161

Andean borders
162

Kachina
163

European borders
164-167

Paisley
168

Tudor rose
169

Folk art bird
170

Australian
borders **171**

Australian
kangaroo **172**

Australian
turtle **173**

Fine Art

Abstraction
175

Optical black
& white **176**

Cubist face
177

Expressionist
faces **178–179**

Pop art
180

Art Nouveau
pattern **181**

Art Nouveau iris
182

Impressionism
183

Bayeux tapestry
184

Icon
185

Japanese wave
186

Samurai
187

Zodiac

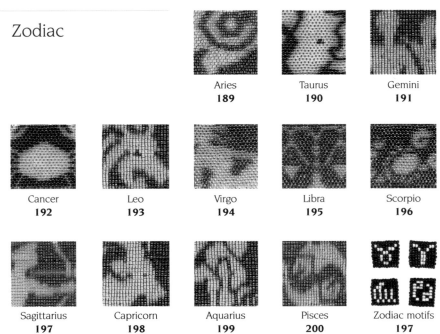

Aries
189

Taurus
190

Gemini
191

Cancer
192

Leo
193

Virgo
194

Libra
195

Scorpio
196

Sagittarius
197

Capricorn
198

Aquarius
199

Pisces
200

Zodiac motifs
197

Alphabets and Numbers

Art Deco **203–209**

Art Deco numbers **210–212**

Small alphabet **217**

Small numbers **227**

Celebrations

Champagne
219

Birthday cake
220

Balloons
221

Graduation
222

Key to the door
223

Christmas tree
224

Bauble
225

Christmas
pudding **226**

Father Christmas
227

Robin
228

New home
229

Heart wreath
230

Wedding cake
231

Horseshoe
232

Rattle
233

Teddy bear
234

Trophy
235

Rocket
236

Catherine
wheel **237**

Pumpkin
238

Shamrock
239

Celebrations
borders **240–241**

Small celebrations
242–243

GEOMETRICS

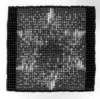

The regular layout of the beads, due to the way the stitches are formed, lends itself very well to geometric patterns. As well as using the designs in this chapter, look through textile patterns and at nature (such as stars and snowflakes) for your inspiration.

Quilt Block

Quilting blocks are a great source of inspiration for patterns, as they are based on simple geometric shapes. If you have a large area of one color, make it more interesting by using a mix of beads of similar colors to fill it in, e.g. you could use a mix of pale blues for the background here.

Smaller than actual size

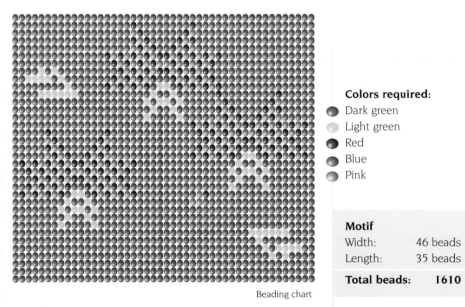

Beading chart

Colors required:
- Dark green
- Light green
- Red
- Blue
- Pink

Motif	
Width:	46 beads
Length:	35 beads
Total beads:	**1610**

Geometric Borders

To extend these patterns to the length you need, simply start at the beginning each time you reach the end of the pattern. You can then use these to make bracelets, chokers, and napkin rings.

Actual size

Beading charts

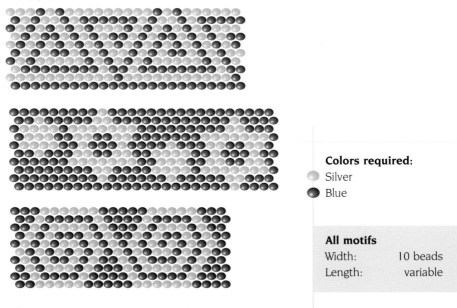

Colors required:

Silver

Blue

All motifs

Width:	10 beads
Length:	variable

If you want to use these borders across the top or bottom of another piece woven with square stitch or on a loom, then simply turn the patterns on their sides. To continue these patterns, just go back to the beginning of the pattern once you reach the end.

Actual size

Beading charts

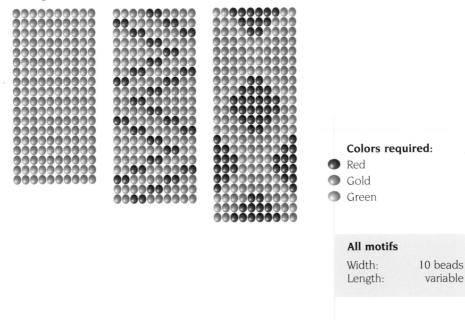

Colors required:
- Red
- Gold
- Green

All motifs

Width:	10 beads
Length:	variable

Small Geometric Patterns

These small patterns are fun to use on their own to decorate greetings cards or pictures, or try linking them with a couple of rows of another color in between to make a bracelet.

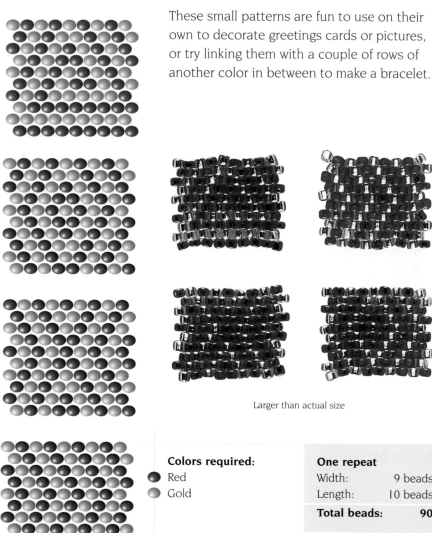

Larger than actual size

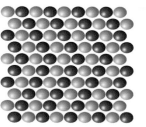

Colors required:

● Red
○ Gold

One repeat

Width:	9 beads
Length:	10 beads
Total beads:	**90**

Beading charts

More small patterns, but this time using square stitch or the loom. Repeat a pattern to make a bracelet or napkin ring, and try a different colorway for a new look.

Beading charts

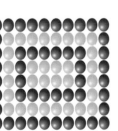

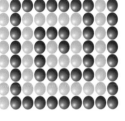

Larger than actual size

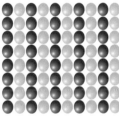

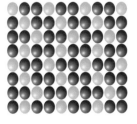

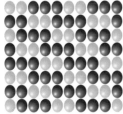

Colors required:

● Blue

○ Silver

One repeat	
Width:	8 beads
Length:	10 beads
Total beads:	**90**

Kathmandu

The textiles of the Himalayan foothills use bright colors and geometric patterns to create eye-catching designs.

Motif

Width:	46 beads
Length:	36 beads

Total beads: 1610

Smaller than actual size

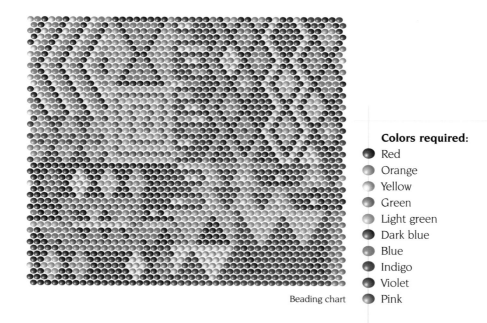

Beading chart

Colors required:
- Red
- Orange
- Yellow
- Green
- Light green
- Dark blue
- Blue
- Indigo
- Violet
- Pink

Star

Use silver-lined beads to make this star really glow. The way the colors fall makes the shape appear almost three-dimensional.

Smaller than actual size

Colors required:

- Red
- Orange
- Gold
- Dark blue
- Light blue
- Silver
- Black
- Dark purple
- Light purple

Motif

Width:	46 beads
Length:	35 beads
Total beads:	**1610**

Beading chart

Woven Diamond

This pattern is designed in the complementary colors of blue and orange, along with red and green. To really make this pattern zing, add a fringe or border in the other two complementary colors, yellow and purple. For a more subtle effect swap this for co-ordinating colors, e.g. two shades of green and two shades of blue.

Actual size

Beading chart

Colors required:
- Green
- Red
- Blue
- Orange

Motif	
Width:	28 beads
Length:	25 beads
Total beads:	**700**

Maze

This symmetrical pattern woven in three colors is sure to draw the eye, and it is a great size for amulet bags.

Larger than actual size

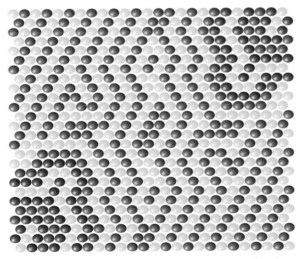

Beading chart

Colors required:

- Dark blue
- Light blue
- Red

Motif	
Width:	25 beads
Length:	26 beads
Total beads:	**650**

Peruvian

Inspired by the brightly colored and geometrically based patterns used for decoration in South America. Use your brightest beads for this pattern!

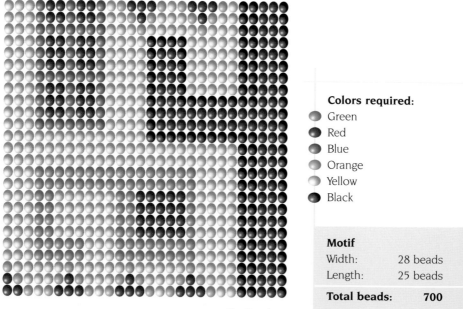

Actual size

Beading chart

Colors required:
- Green
- Red
- Blue
- Orange
- Yellow
- Black

Motif
Width:	28 beads
Length:	25 beads

| **Total beads:** | **700** |

Rainbow

This colorful pattern of rainbow diamonds lends a bit of pizzazz to your work, and lets you show off the range of beads you've been hoarding.

Larger than
actual size

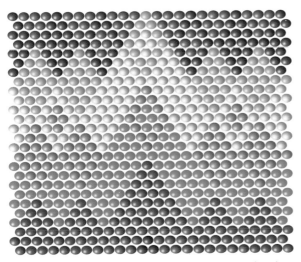

Beading chart

Colors required:

- Red
- Orange
- Yellow
- Green
- Blue
- Indigo
- Violet

Motif

Width:	25 beads
Length:	26 beads
Total beads:	**650**

Snowfall

The snowflakes falling against a dark sky would make a great bag. When you reach the end of the border pattern start again at the beginning until it's the length you require.

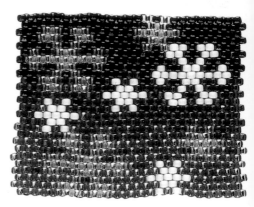

Smaller than actual size

Beading chart

Colors required:
- Very dark blue
- Dark blue
- Blue
- Silver
- White

Motif

Width:	25 beads
Length:	26 beads

Total beads: 650

Snowflake

Who didn't spend winter at school cutting out paper snowflakes? Their six-sided symmetry makes them perfect for inclusion in this chapter. Why not use silver-lined and frosted beads for this piece, to remind you of those winter days?

Smaller than actual size

Beading chart

Colors required:
- Blue
- Silver
- White

Motif

Width:	25 beads
Length:	26 beads

Total beads:	**650**

FLOWERS
AND LEAVES

 Here is a whole garden of flowers, fruits, and leaves for you to weave. Use the border patterns to make bracelets or necklaces, or as an edge to one of the larger patterns. Or pick out your favorite flower and weave a picture.

Flower Basket

Dark brown beads on
the basket base and
handle give form and
dimension to this sweet
motif. You could use
this for amulet bags
and curtain tiebacks.

Actual
size

Beading chart

Colors required:
- Very light green
- Light green
- Dark green
- Light brown
- Dark brown
- Pink
- Red
- Purple
- Light blue
- Dark blue

Motif

Width:	25 beads
Length:	26 beads
Total beads:	**650**

Floral Borders

To use these borders across the top or bottom of another piece woven in square stitch or on a loom, turn the patterns on their sides. To repeat the design, return to the start of the pattern once you reach the end.

▼ Turn book sideways so this becomes the bottom left corner

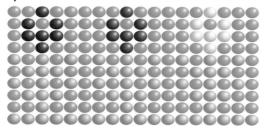

Colors required:
Garden flowers
- Pale blue
- Green
- Red
- Blue
- Yellow

Beading chart

Actual size

Colors required:
Daisies
- Blue
- White
- Yellow
- Green

Actual size

All motifs	
Width:	10 beads
Length:	variable

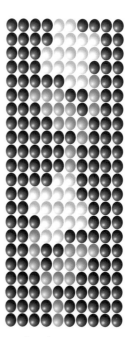

Beading chart

Beading chart

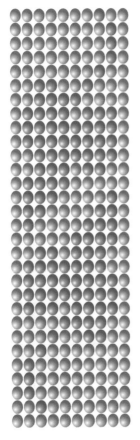

Actual size

Beading chart

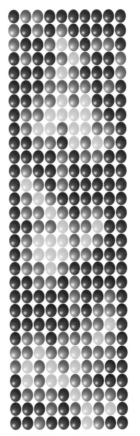

Actual size

Colors required:
Ivy leaves
○ Gold
● Dark green

Colors required:
Variegated ivy
● Dark red
○ Dark green
○ Very pale green

To extend these patterns to the length you need, simply start at the beginning each time you reach the end of the pattern. You can then use these to make bracelets, chokers, and napkin rings.

All motifs
Width: 10 beads
Length: variable

Beading chart

Colors required:
Poppy and cornflower
⬤ White
⬤ Green
⬤ Red
⬤ Black
⬤ Pale blue
⬤ Yellow

Actual size

Actual size

Colors required:
Berries
⬤ Blue
⬤ Light green
⬤ Dark green
⬤ Dark red
⬤ Red
⬤ Light red
⬤ White
⬤ Brown

Turn the book sideways so this becomes the bottom left corner

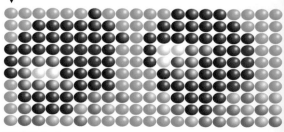

Beading chart

Beading chart

Colors required:
Forget-me-not

- Red
- Yellow
- Light green
- Dark blue
- Light blue

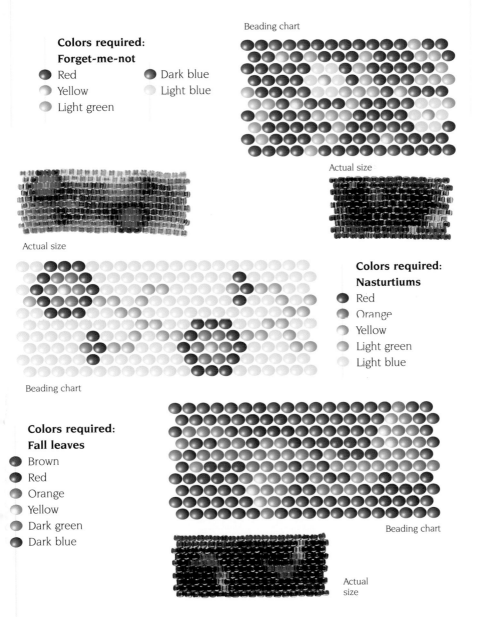

Actual size

Actual size

Colors required:
Nasturtiums

- Red
- Orange
- Yellow
- Light green
- Light blue

Beading chart

Colors required:
Fall leaves

- Brown
- Red
- Orange
- Yellow
- Dark green
- Dark blue

Beading chart

Actual size

Daffodil

This daffodil would make a lovely amulet bag for spring, or mount it on thin colored cardboard to make an Easter greeting card.

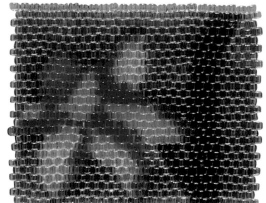

Larger than actual size

Beading chart

Colors required:
- Dark green
- Light green
- Blue
- Dark orange
- Light orange
- Yellow

Motif

Width:	25 beads
Length:	26 beads
Total beads:	**650**

Jasmine

Jasmine is a delicate flower, so weave this pretty design with beads in frosted and transparent colors to emphasize these qualities.

Larger than actual size

Beading chart

Colors required:

- Dark green
- Green
- Light green
- White
- Brown
- Orange
- Yellow
- Gray

Motif

Width:	28 beads
Length:	25 beads

Total beads: **700**

Sunflower

The sunflower is an ever-popular motif and this bright flower will bring the sun into any room.

Smaller than actual size

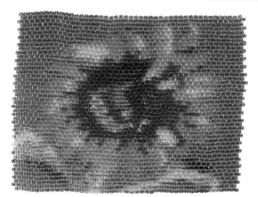

Motif

Width:	45 beads
Length:	46 beads
Total beads:	**2070**

Beading chart

Colors required:

- Orange
- Dark yellow
- Bright yellow
- Dark green
- Light green
- Blue
- Brown
- Light brown
- Dark brown

Pansy

Pansies come in such
fantastic colors that
you can enjoy yourself
picking out all the really
vivid colors from your
store of beads.

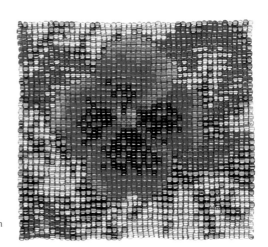

Smaller than
actual size

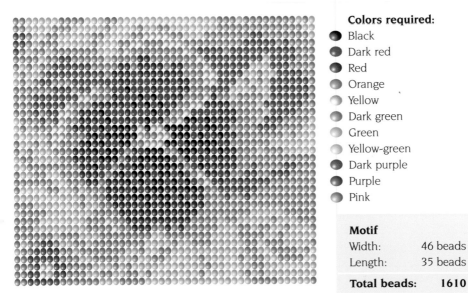

Beading chart

Colors required:

- Black
- Dark red
- Red
- Orange
- Yellow
- Dark green
- Green
- Yellow-green
- Dark purple
- Purple
- Pink

Motif

Width:	46 beads
Length:	35 beads
Total beads:	**1610**

Violets

These delicate violets would
make a lovely amulet bag,
perfect for evening wear.

Actual
size

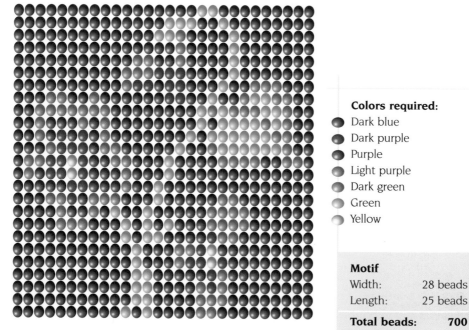

Beading chart

Colors required:
- Dark blue
- Dark purple
- Purple
- Light purple
- Dark green
- Green
- Yellow

Motif

Width: 28 beads
Length: 25 beads

Total beads: 700

Lily

An elegant pure white
lily needs a strong
background color, such
as this vibrant shade
of blue, to set it off.

Smaller than actual size

Beading chart

Colors required:
- Dark green
- Green
- Light green
- Blue
- White
- Gray
- Orange

Motif

Width:	25 beads
Length:	26 beads
Total beads:	**650**

Rose

The black background makes this red rose stand out dramatically. This motif is ideal for framing as a picture or using on a bag.

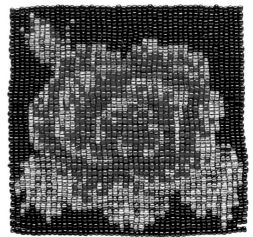

Smaller than actual size

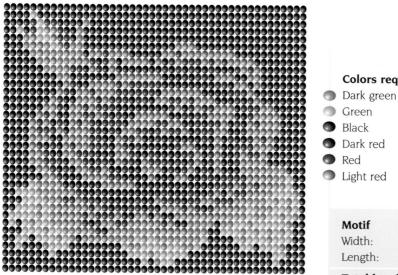

Beading chart

Colors required:
- Dark green
- Green
- Black
- Dark red
- Red
- Light red

Motif

Width:	46 beads
Length:	35 beads
Total beads:	**1610**

Berries

Photographs can often
provide inspiration for
patterns, like this one
of ripe garden berries
and leaves. This
pattern will work well
in a picture frame.

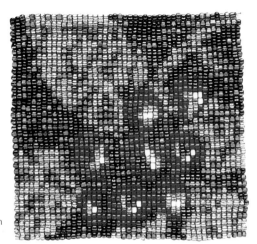

Smaller than
actual size

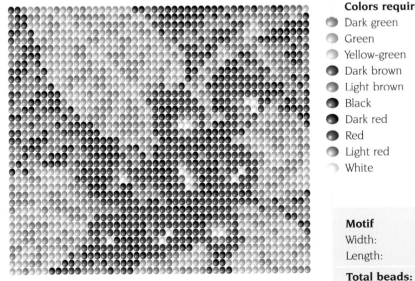

Beading chart

Colors required:
- Dark green
- Green
- Yellow-green
- Dark brown
- Light brown
- Black
- Dark red
- Red
- Light red
- White

Motif

Width:	46 beads
Length:	35 beads
Total beads:	**1610**

Pear

This juicy pear looks
good enough to eat.
You could also weave
this fruit in varying
shades of green.

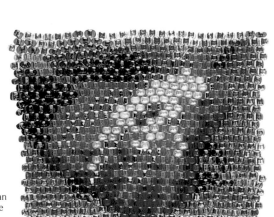

Larger than
actual size

Beading chart

Colors required:
- Red-brown
- Red
- Orange
- Gold
- Cream
- Dark green
- Light green
- Blue

Motif

Width:	25 beads
Length:	26 beads
Total beads:	**650**

Apple

You could add extra interest to this picture of an apple by mixing shades of pale blue to use for the background.

Motif
Width: 45 beads
Length: 46 beads

Total beads: 2070

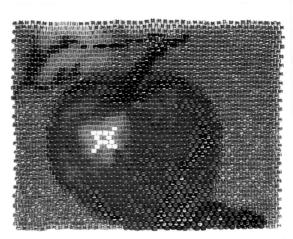

Smaller than actual size

Beading chart

Colors required:
- Light blue
- Dark blue
- Very dark blue
- Dark green
- Light green
- Yellow
- Orange
- Purple
- Light red
- Dark red
- Light brown
- Dark brown
- White
- Black

Small Motifs

These miniature flower motifs are ideal for mounting on a greetings card, or repeat them to make a bracelet.

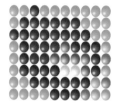

Colors required:
Berry
- Light blue
- White
- Light red
- Dark red
- Red
- Brown
- Light green
- Dark green

Colors required:
Flower vase
- Light blue
- Blue
- Red
- Yellow
- Light green
- Dark green
- Brown

Colors required:
Forget-me nots
- Dark green
- Light green
- Light blue
- Yellow

Berry

Flower vase

All samples actual size

Forget-me nots

Tulip

Colors required:
Tulip
- Light blue
- Orange
- Dark green

Motif	Peyote	Square
Width:	9 beads	10 beads
Length:	10 beads	8 beads
Total beads:	**90**	**80**

Strawberries

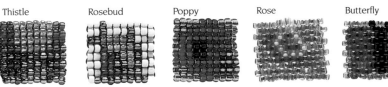

Thistle   Rosebud   Poppy   Rose   Butterfly

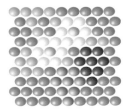

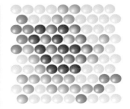

Colors required:
Strawberries
- Blue
- Red
- Light red
- Yellow
- White
- Light green

Colors required:
Rosebud
- Dark green
- Light green
- Red
- White
- Light red

Colors required:
Rose
- Light blue
- Blue
- Red
- Light red
- Yellow
- Light green

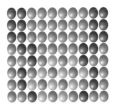

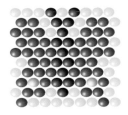

Colors required:
Thistle
- Blue
- Purple
- Dark green
- Light green

Colors required:
Poppy
- Dark green
- Light green
- Red
- Black

Colors required:
Butterfly
- Light blue
- Black
- Red
- Yellow

FUR AND FEATHERS

Here is a parade of domestic, barnyard, and wild animals for you to choose from. You can easily adapt the charts and the colors of beads to weave a picture of your own pet, or go wild with one of the comical cartoon animals.

Jaguar

In only three colors,
this dramatic jungle
scene of a jaguar
silhouetted against
a full moon is
deceptively simple.

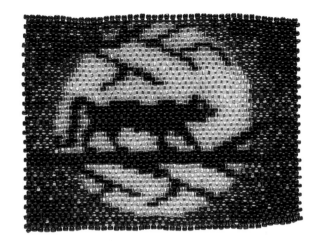

Smaller than actual size

Beading chart

Colors required:
- Black
- Silver
- Dark blue

Motif

Width:	45 beads
Length:	46 beads
Total beads:	**2070**

Cat

A young tabby cat peers out at you from this piece of beadwork, and would look lovely on an amulet bag. You could even add a fringe with a mouse bead in it.

Larger than actual size

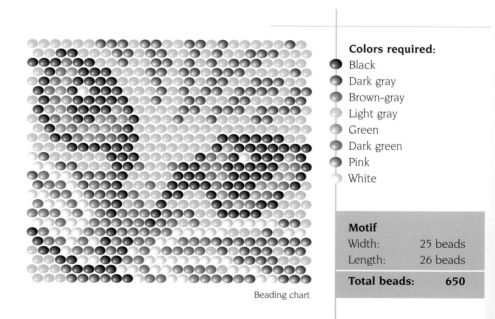

Beading chart

Colors required:
- Black
- Dark gray
- Brown-gray
- Light gray
- Green
- Dark green
- Pink
- White

Motif	
Width:	25 beads
Length:	26 beads
Total beads:	**650**

Scottie Dog

A cute Scottie dog on a plaid background. If you prefer Westies, then swap the black beads for white ones, and use a black bead for his eye.

Actual size

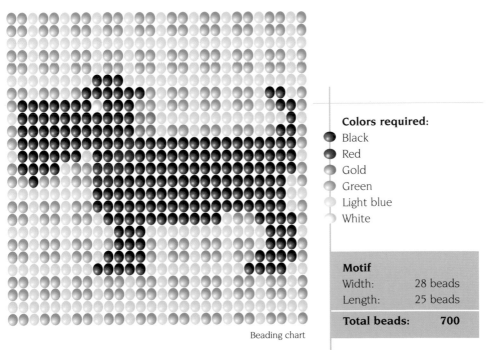

Beading chart

Colors required:
- Black
- Red
- Gold
- Green
- Light blue
- White

Motif

Width:	28 beads
Length:	25 beads
Total beads:	**700**

Cartoon Cat

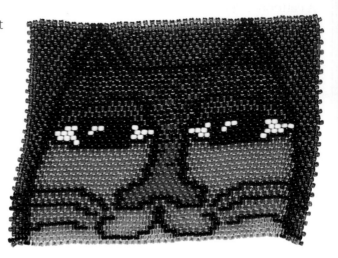

This colorful cat will draw comment whatever you do with it! Use children's books and comics for inspiration.

Smaller than actual size

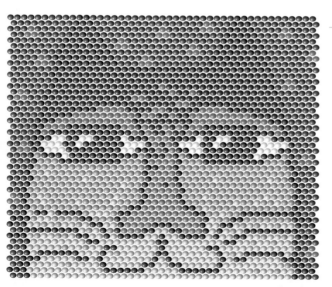

Beading chart

Colors required:
- Red
- Orange
- Gold
- Yellow
- Purple
- Teal
- White
- Black

Motif
Width:	45 beads
Length:	46 beads

Total beads: 2070

Cartoon Dog

A cartoon dog in eye-popping colors. When weaving cartoon characters, you can make the colors as bright and unrealistic as you wish.

Smaller than
actual size

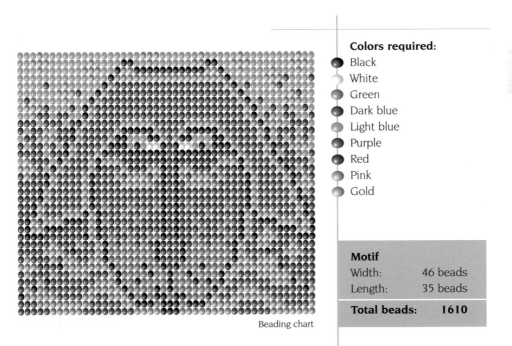

Colors required:

- Black
- White
- Green
- Dark blue
- Light blue
- Purple
- Red
- Pink
- Gold

Beading chart

Motif	
Width:	46 beads
Length:	35 beads
Total beads:	**1610**

Cow

This peaceful pastoral scene of a cow grazing would look good as a framed picture.

Smaller than
actual size

Colors required:

- White
- Pale blue
- Blue
- Dark blue
- Black
- Gray
- Tan
- Dark green
- Light green
- Yellow
- Red

Beading chart

Motif	
Width:	45 beads
Length:	46 beads
Total beads:	**2070**

Pig

This cheerful pig in a
field of daisies will
make a welcome
addition to any farm.
Use him for pictures
or a large amulet bag.

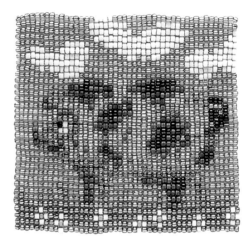

Smaller than
actual size

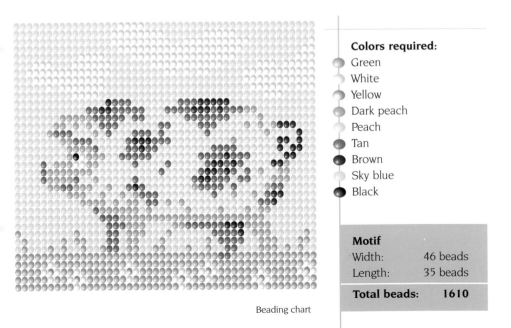

Beading chart

Colors required:

- Green
- White
- Yellow
- Dark peach
- Peach
- Tan
- Brown
- Sky blue
- Black

Motif	
Width:	46 beads
Length:	35 beads
Total beads:	**1610**

Owl

This wise tawny owl
woven in three
shades of brown
would look lovely
as an amulet bag.

Larger than
actual size

Beading chart

Colors required:

- Very dark brown
- Brown
- Light brown
- Black
- Dark blue
- White

Motif	
Width:	25 beads
Length:	26 beads
Total beads:	**650**

Scarlet Macaw

This scarlet macaw shines against its native jungle background and would look lovely stitched in silver-lined beads to give an extra shimmer.

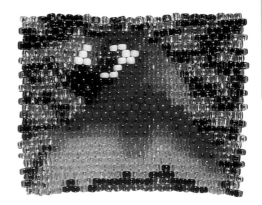

Larger than actual size

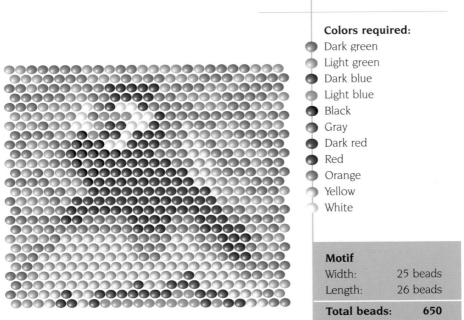

Beading chart

Colors required:
- Dark green
- Light green
- Dark blue
- Light blue
- Black
- Gray
- Dark red
- Red
- Orange
- Yellow
- White

Motif	
Width:	25 beads
Length:	26 beads
Total beads:	**650**

Cockerel

This rooster looks ready
to crow at any moment.
Use iridescent beads for
the blue and green in
his tail for extra effect.

Smaller than
actual size

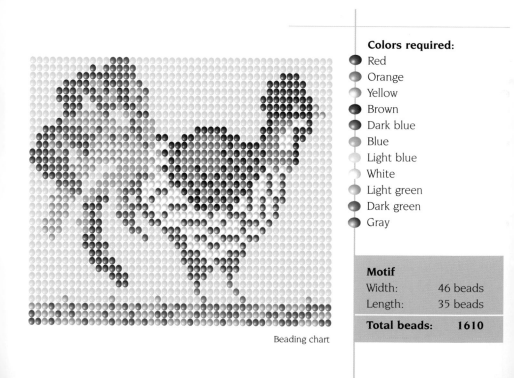

Beading chart

Colors required:

- Red
- Orange
- Yellow
- Brown
- Dark blue
- Blue
- Light blue
- White
- Light green
- Dark green
- Gray

Motif

Width:	46 beads
Length:	35 beads
Total beads:	**1610**

Dove

The classic symbol of peace, this dove looks beautiful when woven in soft, muted colors.

Smaller than actual size

Colors required:

- Black
- Gray
- White
- Red
- Orange
- Yellow
- Dark green
- Light green
- Blue

Motif	
Width:	45 beads
Length:	46 beads
Total beads:	**2070**

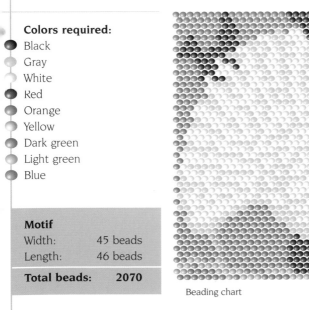

Beading chart

Goose

A comical goose, suitable for a child's amulet bag, or for napkin rings.

Actual size

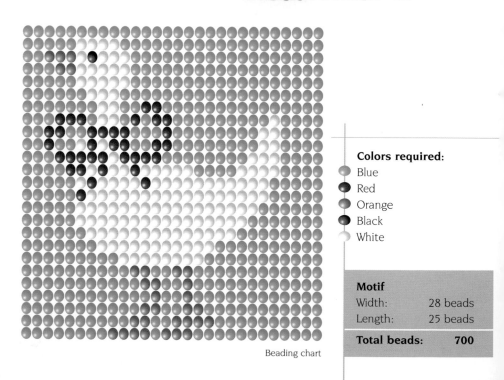

Beading chart

Colors required:

- Blue
- Red
- Orange
- Black
- White

Motif	
Width:	28 beads
Length:	25 beads
Total beads:	**700**

Swan

This serene swan would look great as an amulet with shimmering blue beads for the watery background and with a fluid fringe attached.

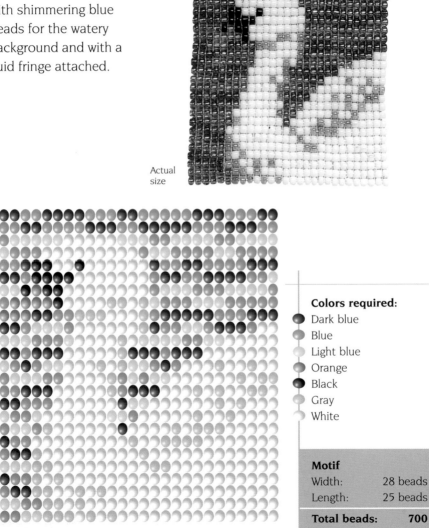

Actual size

Beading chart

Colors required:

- Dark blue
- Blue
- Light blue
- Orange
- Black
- Gray
- White

Motif	
Width:	28 beads
Length:	25 beads
Total beads:	**700**

Indian Elephant

An Indian elephant decked out for a festival. Use your brightest beads for his outfit.

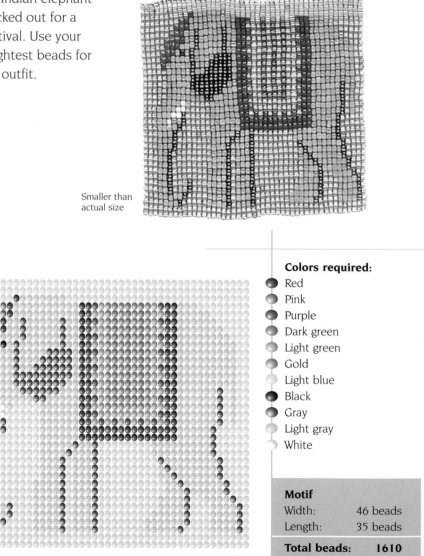

Smaller than actual size

Colors required:

- Red
- Pink
- Purple
- Dark green
- Light green
- Gold
- Light blue
- Black
- Gray
- Light gray
- White

Beading chart

Motif	
Width:	46 beads
Length:	35 beads
Total beads:	**1610**

Zebra

The striking zebra is
fun to stitch. It would
also work well with a
zebra print border
(see page 100).

Actual
size

Beading chart

Colors required:
- Black
- White
- Light blue
- Dark green
- Light green

Motif	
Width:	28 beads
Length:	25 beads
Total beads:	**700**

Animal Borders

When weaving the crocodile, hedgehog, or squirrel, try alternating which way they face. When weaving the zebra stripe (overleaf), if you use golden yellow in place of white, you can turn it into a tiger stripe. To continue these patterns, simply go back to the beginning of the pattern once you reach the end.

▼ Turn book sideways so this becomes the bottom left corner   Beading chart

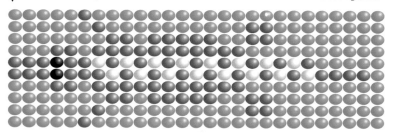

Colors required:
Crocodile
Blue
Dark green
White

Actual size

All motifs
Width: 10 beads
Length: variable

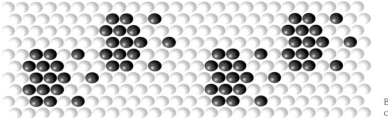

Beading
chart

Colors required:
Pawprints
White
Black

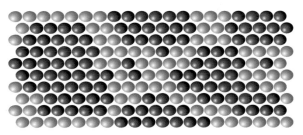

Actual size

Colors required:
Leopard
Black
Golden Yellow
Dark brown

Beading chart

All motifs
Width: 10 beads
Length: variable

Actual
size

Turn the book sideways so this becomes the bottom left corner

▼

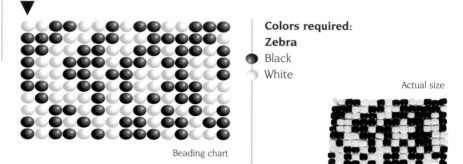

Colors required:
Zebra
● Black
○ White

Beading chart

Actual size

Beading chart

Colors required:
Turtles
● Dark brown
● Light brown
○ Green
○ Light blue

Actual size

Turn the book sideways so this becomes the bottom left corner

▼

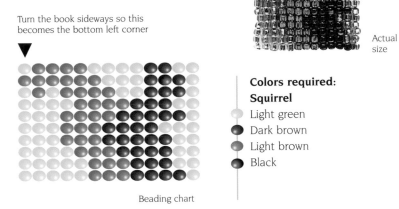

Beading chart

Colors required:
Squirrel

- Light green
- Dark brown
- Light brown
- Black

Actual size

Actual size

Colors required:
Hedgehog

- Dark green
- Dark brown
- Light brown
- Black

▼ Turn book sideways so this becomes the bottom left corner

Beading chart

MARINE

The colors and shapes of the underwater world lend themselves beautifully to the range of beads available. Very effective sea and wave patterns can be created using many shades of blue, while shells and coral make use of pretty pinks and oranges.

Marine Borders

These watery designs are ideal to use as bracelets, edgings, or napkin rings. To continue these patterns, simply go back to the beginning of the chart once you reach the end.

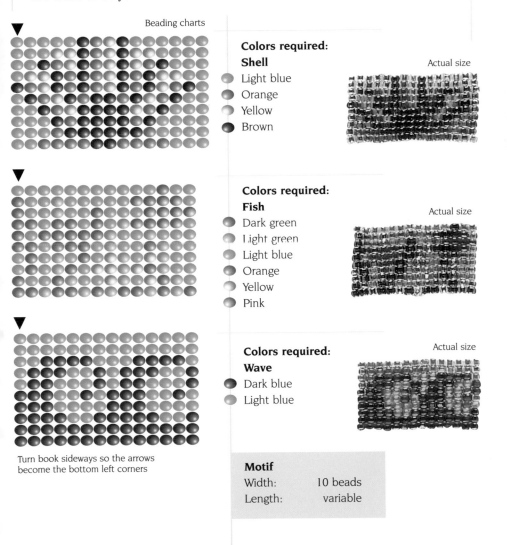

Beading charts

Colors required:
Shell
- Light blue
- Orange
- Yellow
- Brown

Actual size

Colors required:
Fish
- Dark green
- Light green
- Light blue
- Orange
- Yellow
- Pink

Actual size

Colors required:
Wave
- Dark blue
- Light blue

Actual size

Turn book sideways so the arrows become the bottom left corners

Motif
Width: 10 beads
Length: variable

Clown Fish

A clown fish woven
in bright beads,
peeping out from
behind his watery
anemone home.

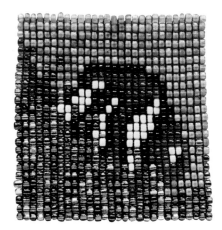

Actual
size

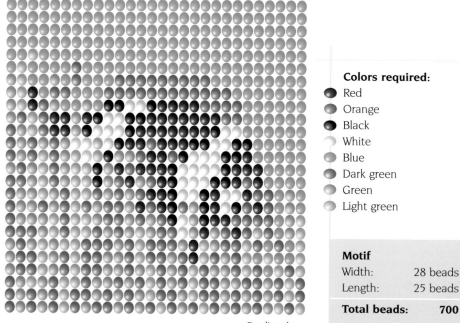

Colors required:

- Red
- Orange
- Black
- White
- Blue
- Dark green
- Green
- Light green

Motif	
Width:	28 beads
Length:	25 beads
Total beads:	**700**

Beading chart

Starfish

A starfish fresh
from the coral reef,
beaded in subtle
shades of pink,
yellow, and orange.

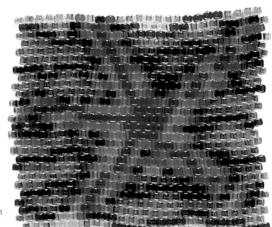

Larger than
actual size

Beading chart

Colors required:
- Dark blue
- Light blue
- Yellow
- Orange
- Pink
- Brown

Motif

Width:	25 beads
Length:	26 beads
Total beads:	**650**

Seahorse

A colorful seahorse
beaded in warm
shades of orange, set
against a rich blue
ocean background.

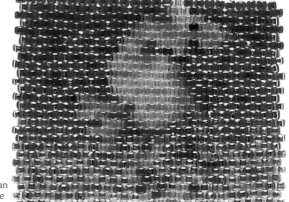

Larger than
actual size

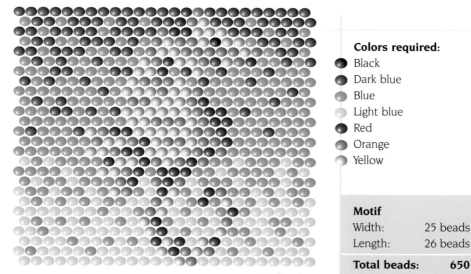

Beading chart

Colors required:

- ● Black
- ● Dark blue
- ● Blue
- ○ Light blue
- ● Red
- ● Orange
- ○ Yellow

Motif

Width:	25 beads
Length:	26 beads

| **Total beads:** | **650** |

Dolphin

Dolphins are always popular, and this cheerful creature would make an attractive amulet bag.

Larger than
actual size

Beading chart

Colors required:
- Black
- Dark gray
- Light gray
- White
- Yellow
- Blue
- Light blue

Motif	
Width:	25 beads
Length:	26 beads
Total beads:	**650**

Seashell

You can almost hear the sea from this beautifully shaded spiraling seashell.

Motif

Width:	45 beads
Length:	46 beads
Total beads:	**2070**

Smaller than actual size

Colors required:

- Green
- Blue
- Cream
- Yellow
- Orange
- Red
- Brown

Beading chart

Small marine motifs

These small patterns are fun to use on their own to decorate greetings cards or pictures, or why not link them together, with a couple of rows of another color in between to make a bracelet?

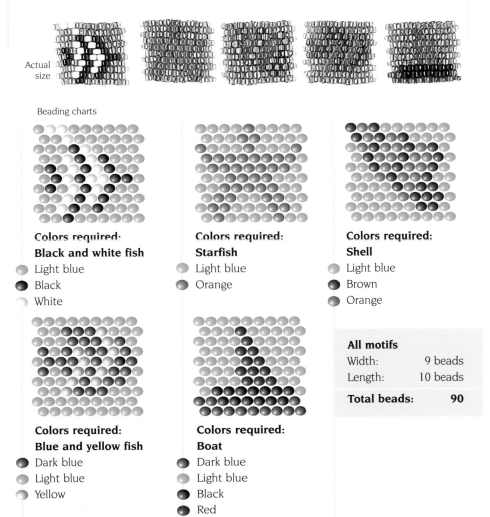

Actual size

Beading charts

Colors required:
Black and white fish
- Light blue
- Black
- White

Colors required:
Blue and yellow fish
- Dark blue
- Light blue
- Yellow

Colors required:
Starfish
- Light blue
- Orange

Colors required:
Boat
- Dark blue
- Light blue
- Black
- Red

Colors required:
Shell
- Light blue
- Brown
- Orange

All motifs	
Width:	9 beads
Length:	10 beads
Total beads:	**90**

Lighthouse

Enjoy weaving this
peaceful scene of
an old-fashioned
lighthouse looking out
over a calm sea.

Smaller than
actual size

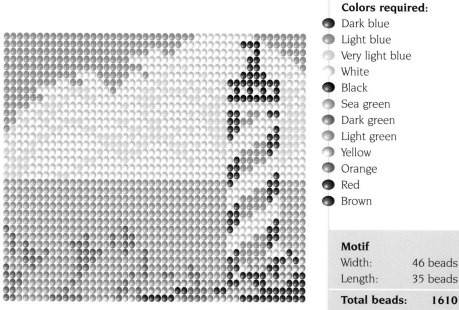

Beading chart

Colors required:
- Dark blue
- Light blue
- Very light blue
- White
- Black
- Sea green
- Dark green
- Light green
- Yellow
- Orange
- Red
- Brown

Motif

Width:	46 beads
Length:	35 beads
Total beads:	**1610**

Boat

A boat with primary-
colored sails cruises by
in this tranquil picture,
while a pair of seagulls
fly overhead.

Smaller than
actual size

Beading chart

Colors required:

- Black
- Dark blue
- Light blue
- White
- Red
- Dark brown
- Light brown

Motif

Width:	46 beads
Length:	35 beads

Total beads: 1610

SEASONS

Here is a collection of borders and motifs for all four seasons. Four of the designs show the same tree throughout the year. You could weave a picture for each season, and frame them as a group, or make a matching set of napkin rings using the border patterns.

The Four Seasons

This is a larger piece showing symbols for the four seasons. You could also weave just one of the seasons for a greetings card or amulet bag.

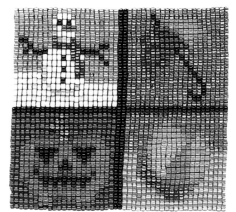

Smaller than
actual size

Beading chart

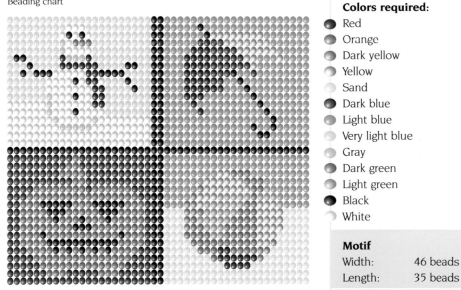

Colors required:

- Red
- Orange
- Dark yellow
- Yellow
- Sand
- Dark blue
- Light blue
- Very light blue
- Gray
- Dark green
- Light green
- Black
- White

Motif

Width:	46 beads
Length:	35 beads
Total beads:	**1610**

Spring

Sunshine is melting the last of the winter snow, and the first blossom is showing in this spring picture.

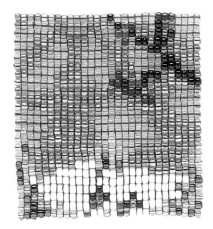

Actual size

Beading chart

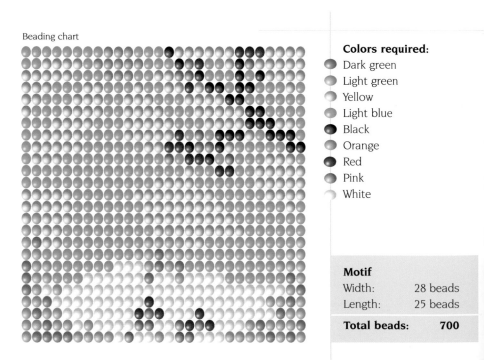

Colors required:
- Dark green
- Light green
- Yellow
- Light blue
- Black
- Orange
- Red
- Pink
- White

Motif	
Width:	28 beads
Length:	25 beads
Total beads:	**700**

Spring Tree

Spring has arrived, and blossom covers the tree, softening the harsh outline of the trunk.

Larger than actual size

Colors required:

- Brown
- Pink
- Peach
- Light blue
- Green
- Gray
- White

Beading chart

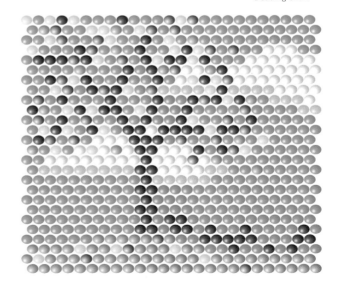

Motif

Width:	25 beads
Length:	26 beads
Total beads:	**650**

Summer

The blazing sun of high summer—this is the perfect design to use beads in the "hot" shades of red, yellow, and orange.

Actual size

Beading chart

Colors required:
- Black
- Red
- Orange
- Yellow
- White

Motif

Width:	28 beads
Length:	25 beads
Total beads:	**700**

Summer Tree

High summer means
shades of green
everywhere, and the
tree is covered with
fresh, new leaves.

Smaller than
actual size

Beading chart

Colors required:

- Brown
- Dark green
- Light green
- Blue
- Red
- Gray
- White

Motif

Width:	25 beads
Length:	26 beads
Total beads:	**650**

Fall

Fall leaves in rich shades
of russet and gold on a
blue background, swirling
in the breeze.

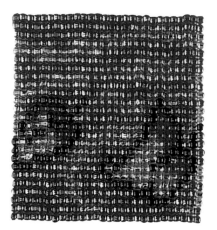

Actual
size

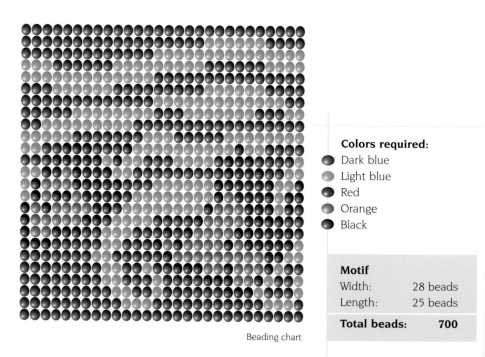

Beading chart

Colors required:

- Dark blue
- Light blue
- Red
- Orange
- Black

Motif	
Width:	28 beads
Length:	25 beads
Total beads:	**700**

Fall Tree

In fall, the tree is stark
and leafless, shown here
against a backdrop of a
stunning sunset.

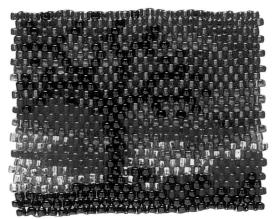

Larger than
actual size

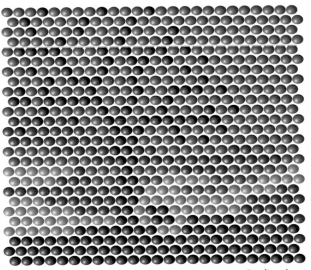

Beading chart

Colors required:
- Black
- Dark blue
- Purple
- Red
- Orange

Motif	
Width:	25 beads
Length:	26 beads
Total beads:	**650**

Winter

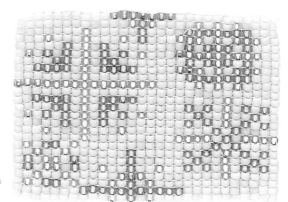

Scandinavian
snowflake designs
in shades of ice give
this winter pattern
a touch of frost.

Larger than
actual size

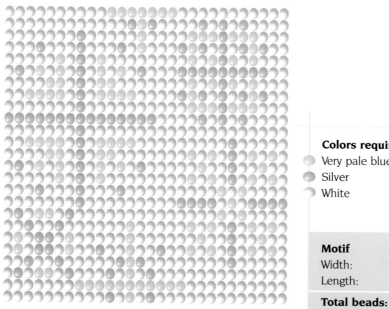

Beading chart

Colors required:
- Very pale blue
- Silver
- White

Motif	
Width:	28 beads
Length:	25 beads
Total beads:	**700**

Winter Tree

A thick blanket of
snow has fallen,
carpeting the tree
in a layer of white.

Larger than
actual size

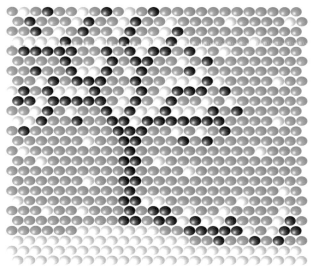

Beading chart

Colors required:
- Brown
- Light blue
- White

Motif	
Width:	25 beads
Length:	26 beads
Total beads:	**650**

Seasonal Borders

A collection of four borders, using the colors and symbols of each season. To extend these patterns to the length you need, simply start at the beginning each time you reach the end of the pattern. You can then use these to make bracelets, chokers, or napkin rings.

Actual size

Colors required: Spring
- Dark green
- Light green
- Yellow

Beading chart

Actual size

Colors required: Summer
- Blue
- Light blue
- Purple
- Yellow
- Pink
- Dark peach
- Peach

Beading chart

Colors required: Fall

- Brown
- Red
- Orange
- Yellow

Actual size

Beading chart

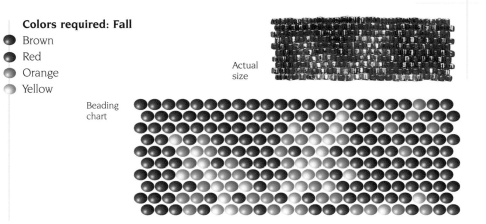

All motifs

Width: variable
Length: 10 beads

Colors required: Winter

- Light blue
- Silver
- White

Actual size

Beading chart

Leaf

This leaf displays all
the brilliant colors
seen in the fall.

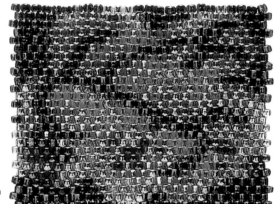

Larger than
actual size

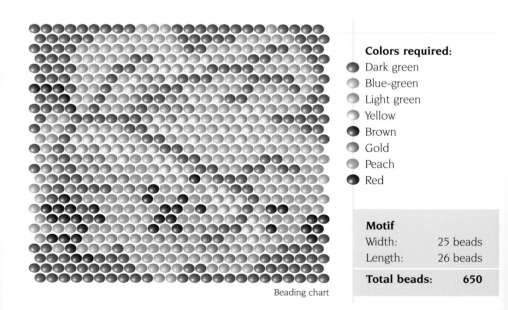

Beading chart

Colors required:
- Dark green
- Blue-green
- Light green
- Yellow
- Brown
- Gold
- Peach
- Red

Motif
Width:	25 beads
Length:	26 beads
Total beads:	**650**

Small Seasonal Motifs

A tree shown through the four seasons. Repeat the pattern to make a bracelet or napkin ring, and try a different colorway for a new look.

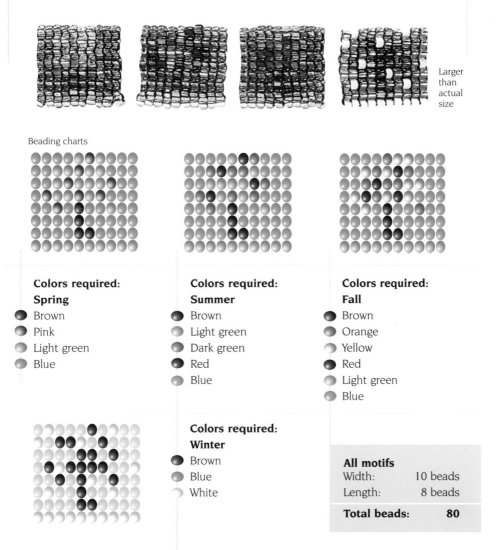

Larger than actual size

Beading charts

Colors required:
Spring
- Brown
- Pink
- Light green
- Blue

Colors required:
Summer
- Brown
- Light green
- Dark green
- Red
- Blue

Colors required:
Fall
- Brown
- Orange
- Yellow
- Red
- Light green
- Blue

Colors required:
Winter
- Brown
- Blue
- White

All motifs
Width: 10 beads
Length: 8 beads

Total beads: 80

CELESTIAL BODIES

Choose colors that are out of this world to weave this stunning range of planetary bodies. These designs would work perfectly for a cosmic bracelet, an amulet bag, or a small framed picture.

Planets

Use this stellar pattern for amulet bags or a picture. This design uses primary colors, but it would look just as effective using a monochrome palette of silver, gray, black, and white.

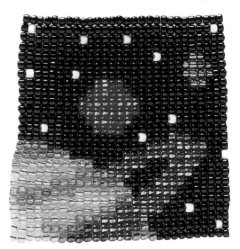

Larger than
actual size

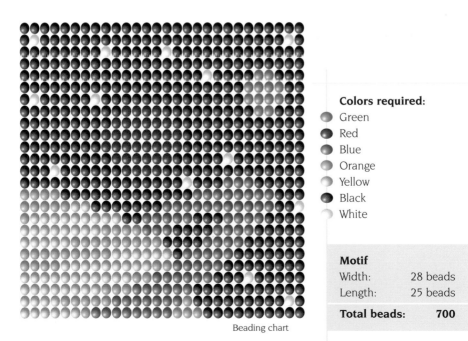

Beading chart

Colors required:

- Green
- Red
- Blue
- Orange
- Yellow
- Black
- White

Motif

Width:	28 beads
Length:	25 beads
Total beads:	**700**

Earthrise

The strong blues and greens of the earth stand out against the starry background. You could use silver beads in place of white for the stars, to add some sparkle to this picture.

Smaller than actual size

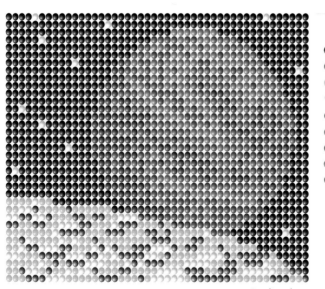

Beading chart

Colors required:
- Black
- Dark gray
- Light gray
- White
- Dark blue
- Light blue
- Dark green
- Light green
- Brown

Motif

Width:	46 beads
Length:	35 beads
Total beads:	**1610**

Moons and Planets Borders

Pick your border from either the phases of the moon or the planets. To extend these patterns to the length you need, simply start at the beginning each time you reach the end of the chart. You can then use them to make bracelets, chokers, or napkin rings.

Actual size

Colors required: Moons
- Black
- Dark blue
- Silver

Beading chart

Actual size

All motifs

Width:	10 beads
Length:	variable

Beading chart

Colors required: Planets
- Black
- Orange
- Yellow
- Light blue
- Green
- Red

Sun

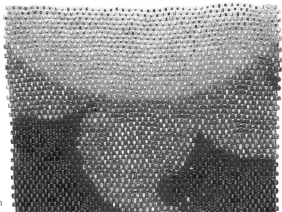

Use glowing silver-lined, brightly colored beads for this slightly abstract modern design of the sun and its rays.

Smaller than actual size

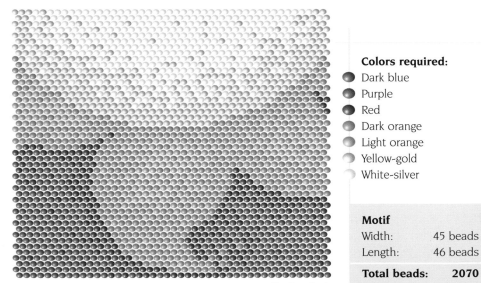

Beading chart

Colors required:
- Dark blue
- Purple
- Red
- Dark orange
- Light orange
- Yellow-gold
- White-silver

Motif

Width:	45 beads
Length:	46 beads

Total beads: **2070**

Moon

Use silver-lined
beads for the
crescent moon
and the stars
to make them
light up the
night sky.

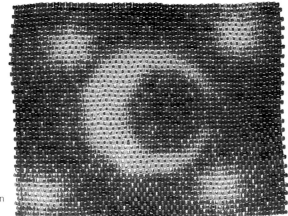

Smaller than
actual size

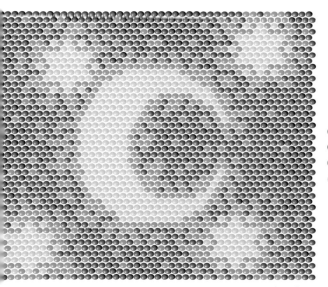

Beading chart

Colors required:
- Very dark blue
- Dark blue
- Blue
- Silver

Motif

Width:	45 beads
Length:	46 beads
Total beads:	**2070**

Sol

A stylized sun
that would look
best woven in
silver-lined beads.

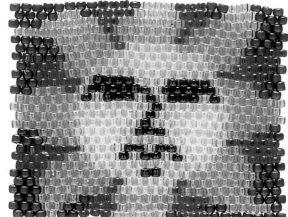

Larger than
actual size

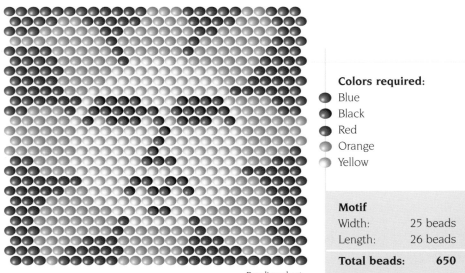

Beading chart

Colors required:
- Blue
- Black
- Red
- Orange
- Yellow

Motif

Width:	25 beads
Length:	26 beads
Total beads:	**650**

Luna

For centuries
people have
associated
legends and folk
tales with the
moon, and the
face visible in it.

Larger than
actual size

Beading chart

Colors required:

- Blue
- Black
- Gray
- Silver

Motif	
Width:	25 beads
Length:	26 beads
Total beads:	**650**

AROUND THE WORLD

In this section you will find a range of patterns based on various world cultures. Many of these designs are large, and would work well as pictures. Alternatively there are some smaller designs that could be used for bracelets or amulet bags.

Celtic Knot

This centuries-old
interlacing band of
Celtic knotwork
makes an eye-
catching pattern.

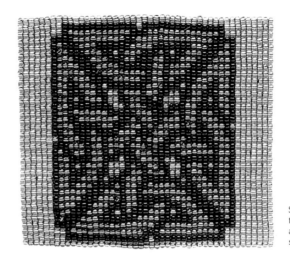

Smaller
than
actual
size

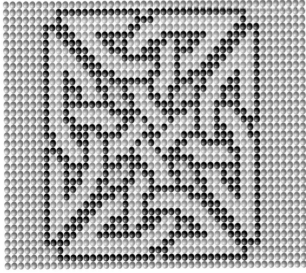

Beading chart

Colors required:
- Black
- Gold
- Green

Motif

Width:	46 beads
Length:	35 beads
Total beads:	**1610**

Celtic Bird

The fantastic animals portrayed in Celtic manuscripts such as the *Book of Kells*, dating from the Dark Ages (roughly 500–1100 AD, from the fall of the Roman Empire to the Middle Ages), were the inspiration for this pattern. Use rich but muted colors to echo the beauty of the original paintings.

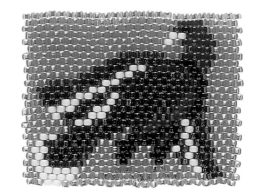

Actual size

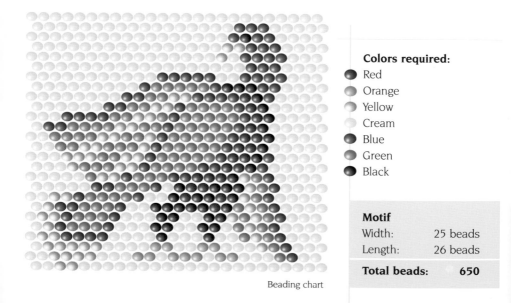

Beading chart

Colors required:
- Red
- Orange
- Yellow
- Cream
- Blue
- Green
- Black

Motif	
Width:	25 beads
Length:	26 beads
Total beads:	**650**

Celtic Spiral

The intricate spirals of
ancient Celtic artwork
provided the inspiration
for this swirling pattern.

Larger
than
actual
size

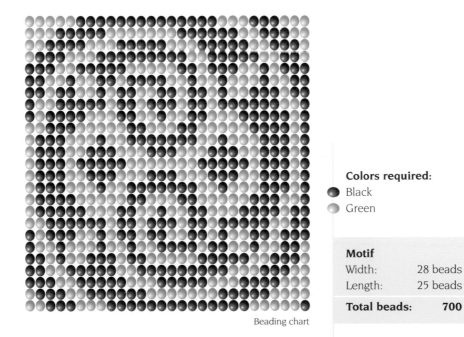

Beading chart

Colors required:
- Black
- Green

Motif

Width:	28 beads
Length:	25 beads
Total beads:	**700**

Celtic Borders

If you want to use these borders across the top or bottom of another piece woven with square stitch or on a loom, simply turn the patterns on their sides. To continue these patterns, go back to the beginning of the pattern once you reach the end.

Beading chart

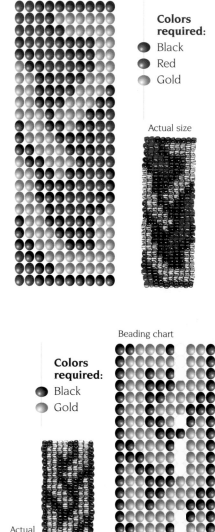

Colors required:

- Black
- Red
- Gold

Actual size

Beading chart

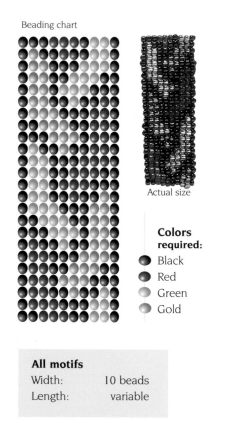

Actual size

Colors required:

- Black
- Red
- Green
- Gold

Colors required:

- Black
- Gold

Beading chart

Actual size

All motifs

Width:	10 beads
Length:	variable

Green Man

The Green Man is an ancient symbol found across Europe, from Ireland to Russia. It is associated with many pre-Christian cultures (including the Celts), but beautiful carved examples can also be found in Christian churches. This piece would look beautiful framed as a picture.

Smaller than actual size

Beading chart

Colors required:

- Dark red
- Brown
- Beige
- Light green
- Dark green
- Pale gray
- Gray-green
- Light blue
- Black

Motif
Width:	45 beads
Length:	46 beads

Total beads: 2070

Japanese Crane

An elegant Japanese crane flying through the sky, with the symbols for Japan worked into the bottom right corner.

Smaller than actual size

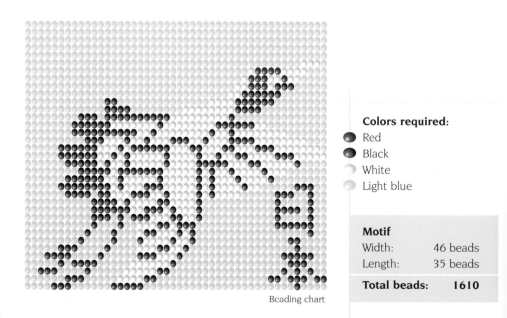

Beading chart

Colors required:

- Red
- Black
- White
- Light blue

Motif

Width:	46 beads
Length:	35 beads

Total beads:	**1610**

Geisha

The carefully made-up
face of a Japanese
geisha features a
stark, white face with
a dramatic slash of
deep red lipstick.

Smaller than
actual size

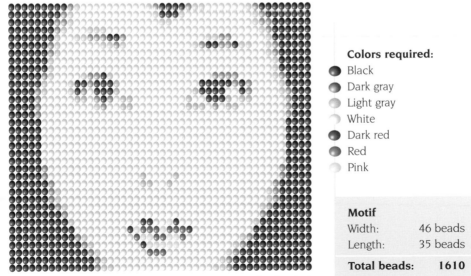

Beading chart

Colors required:
- Black
- Dark gray
- Light gray
- White
- Dark red
- Red
- Pink

Motif	
Width:	46 beads
Length:	35 beads
Total beads:	**1610**

Japanese Tiles

This geometric
design is based
on a traditional
Japanese tile
design known as
Bisyamon-Kikko.

Smaller than
actual size

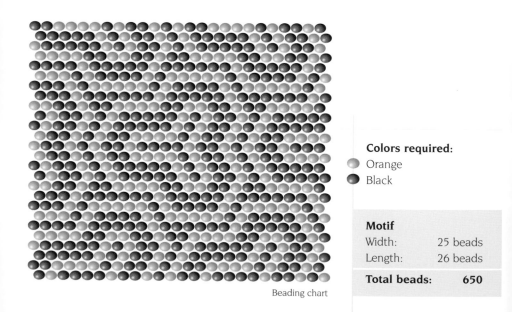

Beading chart

Colors required:
Orange
Black

Motif
Width: 25 beads
Length: 26 beads

Total beads: 650

Japanese Pine

This design is
based on the
traditional symbol
of Japan—the
pine tree.

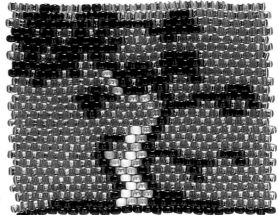

Smaller than
actual size

Beading chart

Colors required:
- Black
- Gray
- White
- Light blue

Motif

Width:	25 beads
Length:	26 beads
Total beads:	**650**

Chinese Dragon

The sinuous forms of
Chinese dragons are a
lot of fun to weave. Use
strong colors to make
it stand out against the
black background.

Smaller than
actual size

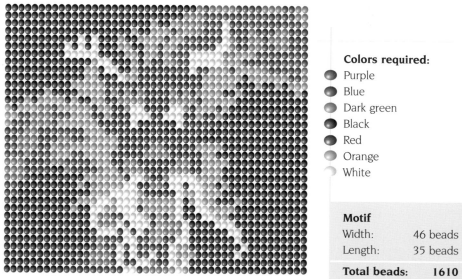

Beading chart

Colors required:

- Purple
- Blue
- Dark green
- Black
- Red
- Orange
- White

Motif

Width:	46 beads
Length:	35 beads

Total beads: 1610

Ginger Jar

The willow pattern
painted onto this
ceramic ginger jar
is a traditional
style of decoration
from China.

Smaller than
actual size

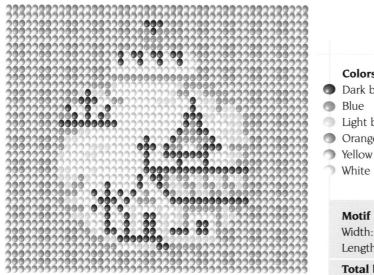

Beading chart

Colors required:

- Dark blue
- Blue
- Light blue
- Orange
- Yellow
- White

Motif

Width: 46 beads
Length: 35 beads

Total beads: 1610

Nepalese Eyes

Pairs of all-seeing eyes are painted onto the towers of the Buddhist temples in Nepal, and are such a strong feature of life that they are becoming a symbol of Nepal.

Smaller than actual size

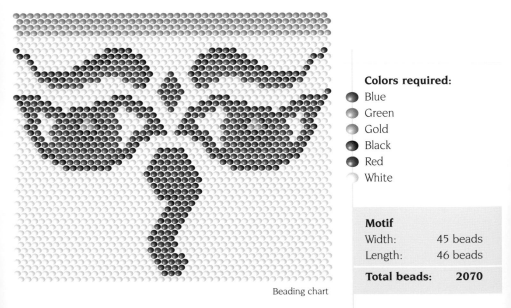

Beading chart

Colors required:
- Blue
- Green
- Gold
- Black
- Red
- White

Motif	
Width:	45 beads
Length:	46 beads
Total beads:	**2070**

Eye of Horus

Horus was the Sun
God of Ancient
Egypt. This symbol
is also known as
the wedjat eye.

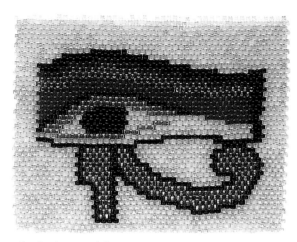

Smaller than actual size

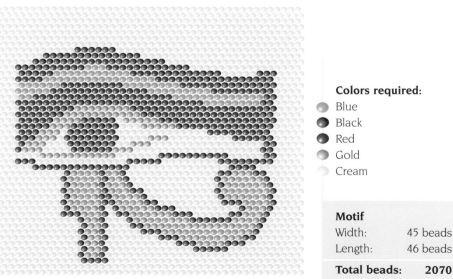

Beading chart

Colors required:
- Blue
- Black
- Red
- Gold
- Cream

Motif

Width:	45 beads
Length:	46 beads
Total beads:	**2070**

Scarab

The ancient Egyptians believed that the Scarab beetle rolled the sun across the sky each day. Amulets were carved into this stylized Scarab form and worn or buried with the dead.

Actual size

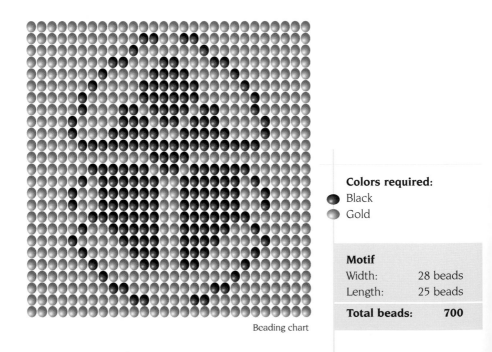

Beading chart

Colors required:
- Black
- Gold

Motif

Width:	28 beads
Length:	25 beads

Total beads:	**700**

African Drummer

An African musician
dressed in brightly
colored robes, beating
a traditional drum.

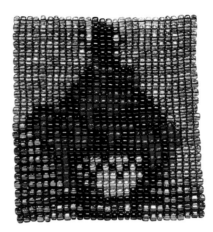

Actual
size

Beading chart

Colors required:
- Black
- Dark blue
- Light blue
- Very pale blue
- Green
- Light brown
- Dark brown
- Red
- Orange

Motif
Width: 28 beads
Length: 25 beads

Total beads: 700

African Textile Pattern

This design was inspired
by the bold, vibrant colors
and geometric shapes of
traditional African textiles.

Larger
than
actual
size

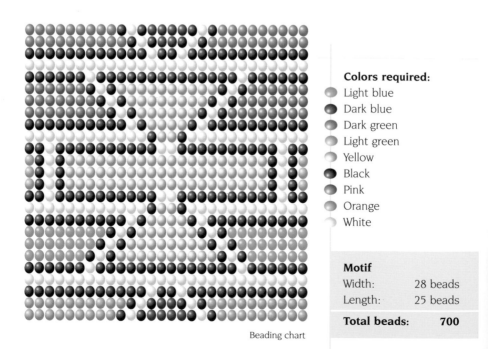

Beading chart

Colors required:
- Light blue
- Dark blue
- Dark green
- Light green
- Yellow
- Black
- Pink
- Orange
- White

Motif

Width: 28 beads
Length: 25 beads

Total beads: 700

African Borders

To use these borders across the top or bottom of another piece woven with square stitch or on a loom, turn the patterns on their sides. To continue these patterns, simply go back to the beginning of the chart once you reach the end.

Beading chart

Colors required:
- Blue
- Black

All motifs

Width:	10 beads
Length:	variable

Smaller than actual size

Beading chart

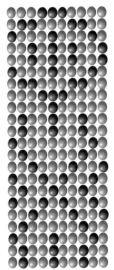

Smaller than actual size

Beading chart

Colors required:
- Orange
- Black

Smaller than actual size

Colors required:
- Pink
- Black

Ontovalo Sun

This cheerful sun is
based on a design by
the Ontovalo Indian
tribe of South America.

Actual
size

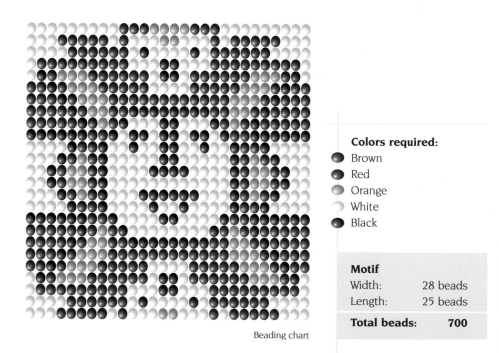

Beading chart

Colors required:
- Brown
- Red
- Orange
- White
- Black

Motif	
Width:	28 beads
Length:	25 beads
Total beads:	**700**

Indian Scrollwork Pattern

This elegant design
is based on the
beautiful patterns
and rich colors of
Indian scrollwork.

Larger than
actual size

Beading chart

Colors required:
- Dark blue
- Light blue
- Light green
- White
- Pink

Motif

Width:	25 beads
Length:	26 beads
Total beads:	**650**

Indian Dancer

An Indian woman
traditionally
dressed in a
brightly colored
sari and gold
jewelry, holding
a lotus blossom.

Smaller than
actual size

Beading chart

Colors required:
- Pink
- Red
- Orange
- Gold
- Light green
- Dark green
- Dark blue
- Light blue
- White
- Black
- Brown

Motif	
Width:	45 beads
Length:	46 beads
Total beads:	**2070**

Las Chismosas

A group of indigenous women sitting in front of the Cotpaxi volcano. This design is typical of the Otovalo Indian tribe of South America, and the colors reflect the natural dyes this would be worked in.

Smaller than actual size

Beading chart

Colors required:

- Black
- Gray
- White
- Brown
- Red
- Orange

Motif

Width:	45 beads
Length:	46 beads
Total beads:	**2070**

Native American Borders

To extend these patterns to the length you need, simply start at the beginning each time you reach the end of the pattern. You can then use them to make bracelets, chokers, or napkin rings.

Beading chart

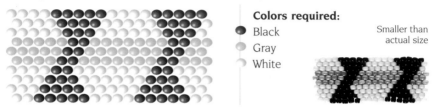

Colors required:

- Black
- Gray
- White

Smaller than actual size

Colors required:

- White
- Blue
- Green
- Red

Smaller than actual size

Beading chart

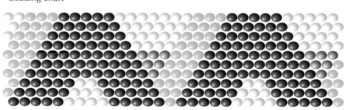

Beading chart

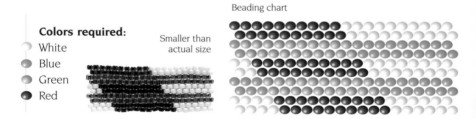

All motifs	
Width:	variable
Length:	10 beads

Colors required:

- Black
- Gray
- White
- Light red

Smaller than actual size

Beading chart

All motifs
Width: 10 beads
Length: variable

Smaller than
actual size

Beading chart

Smaller than
actual size

Colors required:
- Red
- Yellow
- Dark blue
- White

Colors required:
- Brown
- Dark blue
- Light blue
- Green
- White

Colors required:
- Black
- Brown
- White

Smaller than
actual size

Beading chart

Russian Domes

The distinctive
onion-shaped
domes of Moscow
and St. Petersburg
are recognized
around the world.

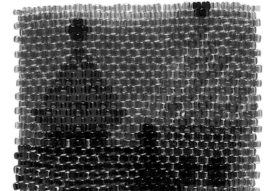

Larger than
actual size

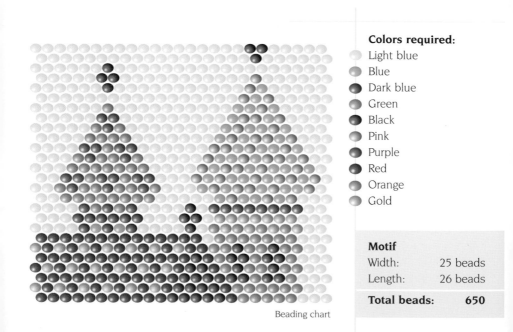

Beading chart

Colors required:
- Light blue
- Blue
- Dark blue
- Green
- Black
- Pink
- Purple
- Red
- Orange
- Gold

Motif

Width:	25 beads
Length:	26 beads
Total beads:	**650**

Cornflower

Much of the traditional art of
Eastern Europe is based on
stylized forms of local flora
and fauna, such as this
delicate blue cornflower.

Actual
size

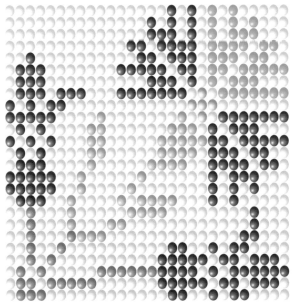

Beading chart

Colors required:
- Dark blue
- Light blue
- White
- Brown
- Dark green
- Light green
- Yellow

Motif	
Width:	28 beads
Length:	25 beads
Total beads:	**700**

Tiszavidék

Embroidery and weaving
in stylized patterns of
red, black, and white are
typical of the traditional
textiles of the Tisza
region of Hungary (the
Tisza is the second
longest river in Hungary).

Smaller than actual size

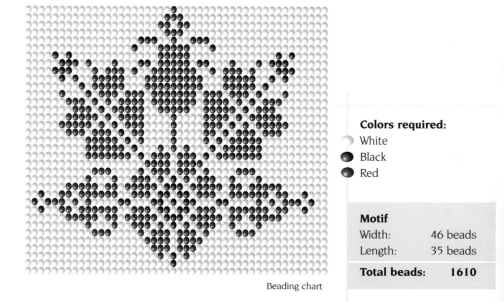

Beading chart

Colors required:
- White
- Black
- Red

Motif	
Width:	46 beads
Length:	35 beads
Total beads:	**1610**

Matyo Embroidery

The stylized leaves
and flowers of Matyo
embroidery can be
found in the region
around the town of
Mezökövesd in Hungary.
The distinctive bright
colors on a black
background give you
the opportunity to go
wild with your beads.

Smaller than actual size

Colors required:
- Pink
- Red
- Orange
- Yellow
- Black
- Light green
- Dark green
- Dark blue
- Light blue

Motif

Width:	45 beads
Length:	46 beads

| **Total beads:** | **2070** |

Beading chart

Andean Borders

These patterns are based on the natural dye colors and geometric patterns of the Otolavo Indian tribe of the Andes. To use across the top or bottom of a piece woven with square stitch or on a loom, turn the patterns on their sides. To continue these patterns, go back to the beginning of the chart once you reach the end.

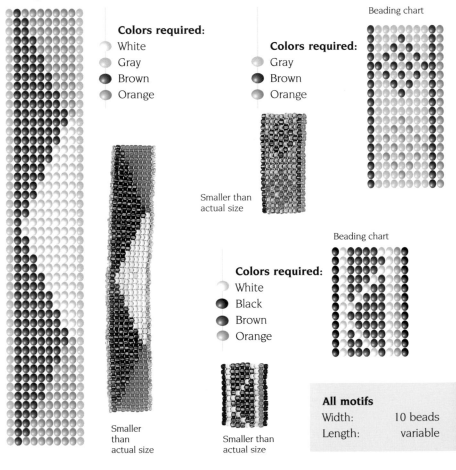

Beading chart

Colors required:
- White
- Gray
- Brown
- Orange

Colors required:
- Gray
- Brown
- Orange

Beading chart

Smaller than actual size

Colors required:
- White
- Black
- Brown
- Orange

Beading chart

Smaller than actual size

Smaller than actual size

All motifs
Width:	10 beads
Length:	variable

Kachina

Kachinas are doll-like
representations of
spirits made by the
Hopi tribe of Native
Americans to educate
their children in the
spiritual world.

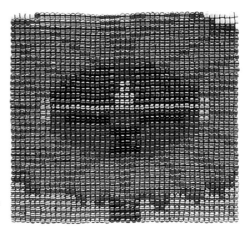

Smaller than
actual size

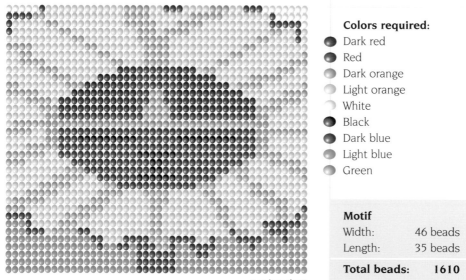

Beading chart

Colors required:
- Dark red
- Red
- Dark orange
- Light orange
- White
- Black
- Dark blue
- Light blue
- Green

Motif	
Width:	46 beads
Length:	35 beads
Total beads:	**1610**

European Borders

The embroidery patterns of Eastern Europe are based on stylized flowers and geometric shapes in bright colors. To extend these patterns to the length required, simply start at the beginning each time you reach the end of the pattern. More borders appear on pages 166–167.

Beading chart

Colors required:
- Blue
- Dark green
- Yellow
- Red

Smaller than actual size

Smaller than actual size

Colors required:
- Black
- Blue
- Light green
- Red
- Pink

Beading chart

Beading chart

Colors required:
- Black
- Blue
- Dark green
- Yellow
- Pink

All motifs

Width:	variable
Length:	10 beads

Smaller than actual size

Beading chart

Colors required:
- Blue
- Dark green
- Red

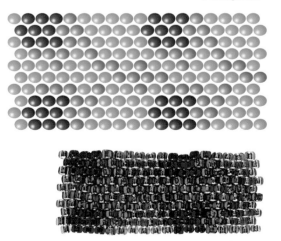

Smaller than actual size

A further selection of European-style borders. These "strip" designs are very adaptable and can be used for bracelets and napkin rings.

Colors required:
- Black
- Red
- Dark green
- White

All motifs

Width: 10 beads
Length: variable

Beading chart

Smaller than actual size

Smaller than actual size

Beading chart

Colors required:
- Black
- Orange
- Yellow
- Light blue

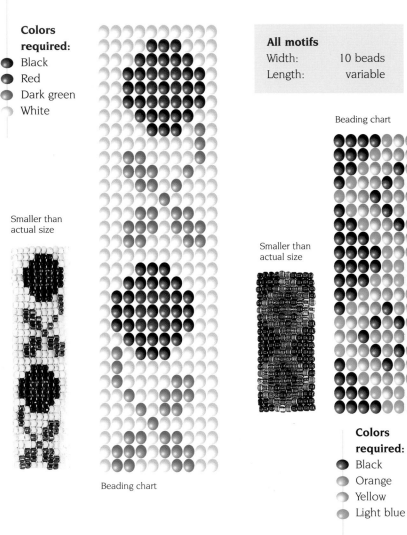

▼ Turn book sideways so this becomes the bottom left corner   Beading chart

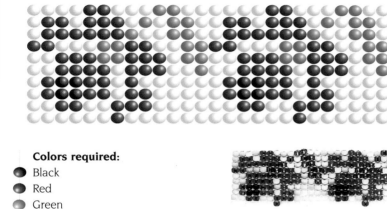

Colors required:
- Black
- Red
- Green
- White

Smaller than
actual size

▼ Turn book sideways so this becomes the bottom left corner   Beading chart

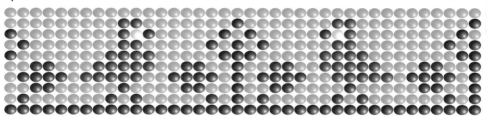

Colors required:
- Brown
- Red
- Dark blue
- Light blue
- White

Smaller than
actual size

Paisley

Variations on this design are typical of those used by the silk industry of Paisley in Scotland since the nineteenth century, and were adapted from the Boteh, a motif used in Indian textiles for centuries.

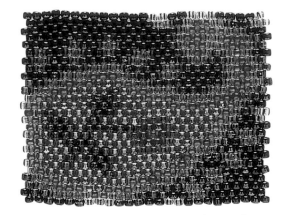

Larger than actual size

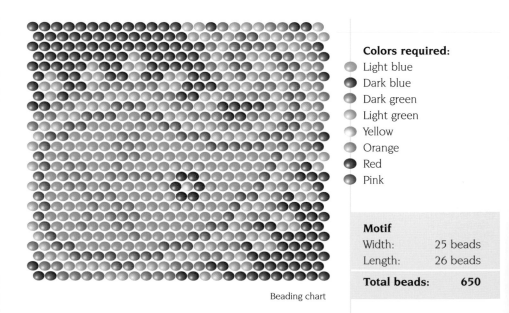

Beading chart

Colors required:
- Light blue
- Dark blue
- Dark green
- Light green
- Yellow
- Orange
- Red
- Pink

Motif

Width:	25 beads
Length:	26 beads
Total beads:	**650**

Tudor Rose

One of the symbols of the English monarchy, the Tudor Rose was formed by combining the white rose of York with the red rose of Lancaster when the two families married to end the fifteenth-century War of the Roses.

Larger than actual size

Beading chart

Colors required:
- Red
- Yellow
- Green
- Blue
- White

Motif	
Width:	25 beads
Length:	26 beads
Total beads:	**650**

Folk Art Bird

This brightly colored bird
on a floral background
is typical of the folk art
embroidery patterns seen
in many Eastern European
countries. Red and black
are often used in these
traditional designs.

Actual
size

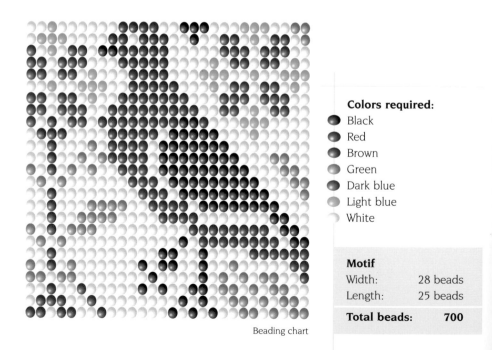

Colors required:
- Black
- Red
- Brown
- Green
- Dark blue
- Light blue
- White

Motif

Width:	28 beads
Length:	25 beads
Total beads:	**700**

Beading chart

Australian Borders

These borders based on Aboriginal dot paintings can easily be extended by returning to the beginning of the pattern once you reach the end.

Beading chart

Smaller than
actual size

Colors required:
- White
- Brown
- Orange

All motifs	
Width:	10 beads
Length:	variable

Beading chart

Beading chart

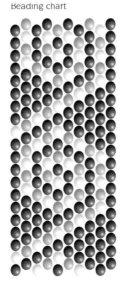

Colors required:
- White
- Black
- Orange

Smaller than
actual size

Colors required:
- Blue
- White
- Brown

Smaller than
actual size

Australian Kangaroo

The Aboriginal tribes in
the deserts of central
Australia use dot or
sand paintings to tell
stories. This intricate
bead pattern is based
on such paintings.

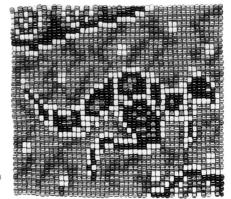

Smaller than
actual size

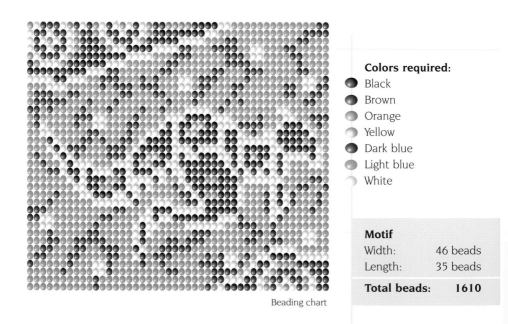

Beading chart

Colors required:
- Black
- Brown
- Orange
- Yellow
- Dark blue
- Light blue
- White

Motif	
Width:	46 beads
Length:	35 beads
Total beads:	**1610**

Australian Turtle

In the dot paintings
of central Australia,
each shape or image
has an allegorical
significance.

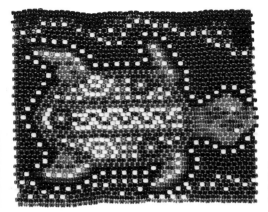

Motif

Width:	45 beads
Length:	46 beads
Total beads:	**2070**

Smaller
than
actual
size

Colors required:
- Black
- Dark brown
- Light brown
- Green
- Dark blue
- Light blue
- White

Beading chart

FINE ART

Art and artists throughout history and across many cultures have provided the inspiration for this range of patterns. Why not weave your very own work of art for your home? See page 250 for advice on framing your beadwork.

Abstract Black and White

This design was inspired
by the work of Wassily
Kandinsky, who is credited
by many as being the first
truly abstract painter.

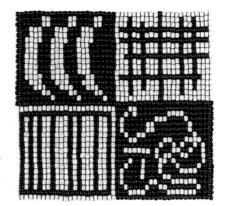

Smaller
than
actual
size

Beading chart

Colors required:

⬭ White
⬤ Black

Motif	
Width:	46 beads
Length:	35 beads
Total beads:	**1610**

Optical Black and White

Modern abstract art has moved away from the representational forms that could still be identified in the work of the expressionists and cubists, instead evoking a response through color and shape.

Actual size

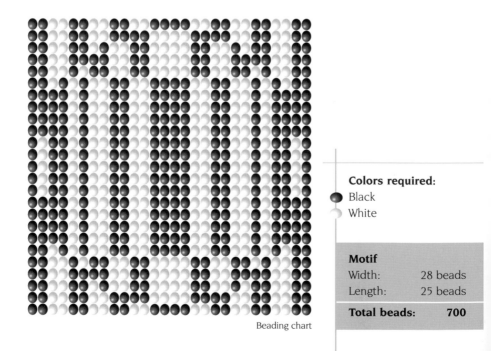

Beading chart

Colors required:
Black
White

Motif	
Width:	28 beads
Length:	25 beads
Total beads:	**700**

Cubist Face

Cubism was developed in
the early twentieth century
by artists Georges Braque
and Pablo Picasso. It was
strongly influenced by tribal
art, and this vivid and
abstract face is typical
of the movement.

Smaller than
actual size

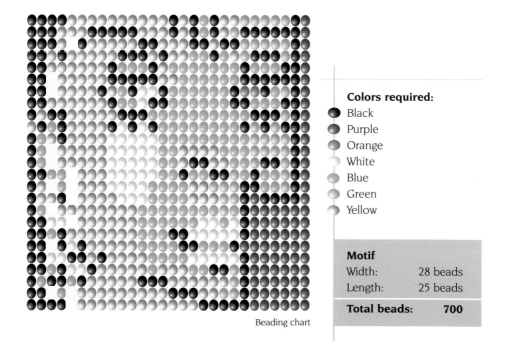

Beading chart

Colors required:
- Black
- Purple
- Orange
- White
- Blue
- Green
- Yellow

Motif	
Width:	28 beads
Length:	25 beads
Total beads:	**700**

Expressionist Faces

The Expressionist movement did not intend to reproduce the subject of the picture accurately, but instead aimed to express the inner state of the artist's mind, as in this vividly colored and highly stylized profile based on the work of well-known expressionist Amedeo Modigliani.

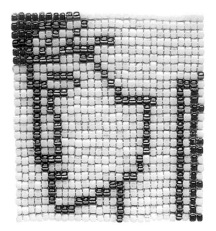

Actual size

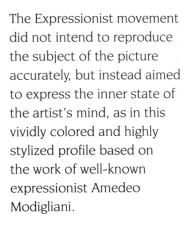

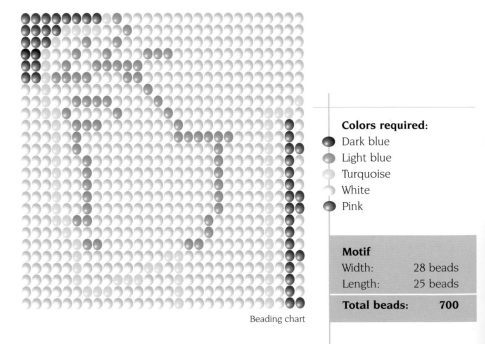

Beading chart

Colors required:
- Dark blue
- Light blue
- Turquoise
- White
- Pink

Motif	
Width:	28 beads
Length:	25 beads
Total beads:	**700**

Expressionist artists such as Paul Klee were highly influenced by tribal and primitive arts. This pattern was inspired by his work.

Actual size

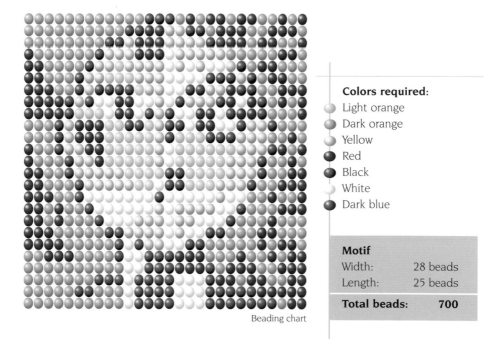

Beading chart

Colors required:
- Light orange
- Dark orange
- Yellow
- Red
- Black
- White
- Dark blue

Motif	
Width:	28 beads
Length:	25 beads
Total beads:	**700**

Pop Art

Pop Art uses bright colors and simple images. Perhaps the best-known artist associated with Pop Art is Andy Warhol, but this picture was inspired by the work of David Hockney.

Smaller than actual size

Motif	
Width:	45 beads
Length:	46 beads
Total beads:	**2070**

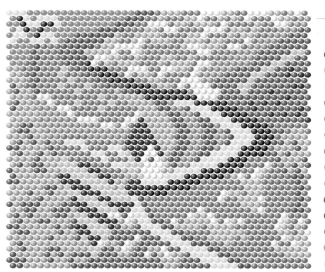

Beading chart

Colors required:
- Black
- Gray
- White
- Turquoise
- Blue
- Dark green
- Green
- Light green
- Sea green
- Brown
- Dark red
- Light red
- Orange
- Yellow

Art Nouveau Pattern

Rich colors, luxuriant areas of pattern, and symbolism formed a major part of the Art Nouveau movement. Gustav Klimt was known for his extravagant paintings and provided the inspiration for this piece in shades of gold and red.

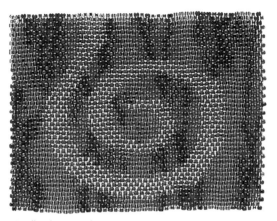

Smaller than actual size

Colors required:
- Gold
- Orange
- Light red
- Red
- Dark red

Motif	
Width:	45 beads
Length:	46 beads
Total beads:	**2070**

Beading chart

Art Nouveau Iris

Nature presented in a stylized form was the basis of the Art Nouveau movement, and can be seen in such work as L.C. Tiffany's stained glass—the inspiration for this pattern.

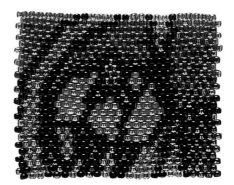

Actual size

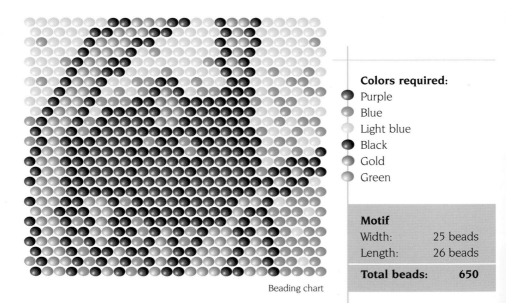

Beading chart

Colors required:

- Purple
- Blue
- Light blue
- Black
- Gold
- Green

Motif	
Width:	25 beads
Length:	26 beads

Total beads:	**650**

Impressionism

Impressionists aimed to give the feeling and effect of their subject without including too much detail. One of the most popular impressionists is Claude Monet, whose work inspired this piece.

Actual size

Beading chart

Colors required:
- Dark pink
- Light pink
- Dark green
- Light green
- Dark blue
- Blue
- Light blue

Motif

Width:	25 beads
Length:	26 beads
Total beads:	**650**

Bayeux Tapestry

The famous Bayeux Tapestry tells the story of the Battle of Hastings in 1066 between the English King Harold and the Norman, William the Conqueror. Choose subtle, natural colors to recall the original embroidery.

Smaller than actual size

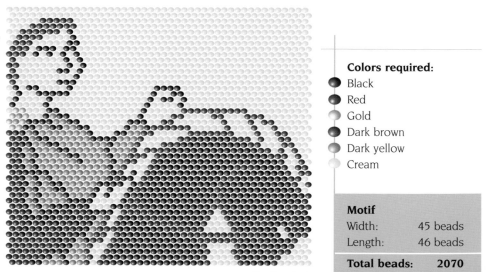

Beading chart

Colors required:

- Black
- Red
- Gold
- Dark brown
- Dark yellow
- Cream

Motif	
Width:	45 beads
Length:	46 beads
Total beads:	**2070**

Icon

Beautiful icons can be found in medieval churches and chapels across much of Europe. You could stitch this piece in soft muted colors to give it an antique look, or in strong glowing colors to give an impression of how these pieces of art looked when new.

Smaller than actual size

Beading chart

Colors required:

- ● Brown
- ● Light brown
- ○ Cream
- ○ White
- ● Black
- ● Dark red
- ● Red
- ○ Gold

Motif	
Width:	45 beads
Length:	46 beads
Total beads:	**2070**

Japanese Wave

The Japanese artist
Hokusai was
particularly famous for
his woodblock prints
portraying water.

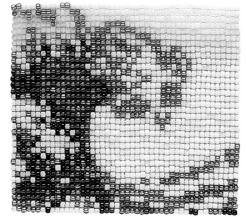

Smaller than
actual size

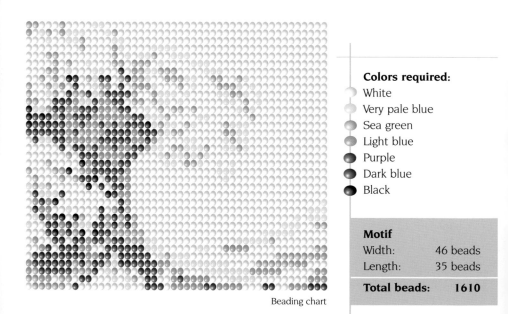

Beading chart

Colors required:

- White
- Very pale blue
- Sea green
- Light blue
- Purple
- Dark blue
- Black

Motif	
Width:	46 beads
Length:	35 beads
Total beads:	**1610**

Samurai

Japanese art focuses
on clean lines and a
limited palette, as in
this striking image of
a samurai warrior.

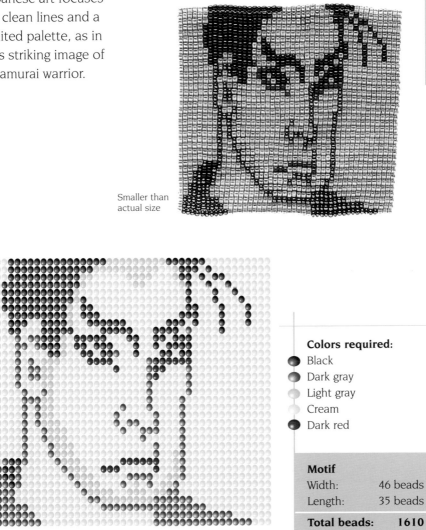

Smaller than
actual size

Beading chart

Colors required:

- Black
- Dark gray
- Light gray
- Cream
- Dark red

Motif	
Width:	46 beads
Length:	35 beads
Total beads:	**1610**

ZODIAC

Do you believe the stars influence your life? In this chapter you will find a pattern for each sign of the zodiac, ideal for amulet bags, pictures, or brooches. You could link all the symbols to make a bracelet, or use them individually on a greeting card.

Aries

The sign of the ram, and a fire sign. People born under Aries are said to be impulsive, energetic, and independent.

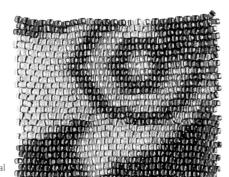

Actual size

Beading chart

Colors required:
- Blue
- Silver

Motif	
Width:	25 beads
Length:	26 beads
Total beads:	**650**

Taurus

This earth sign is represented by a bull, and those born under Taurus are said to be strong-willed, sensual, and hard-working.

Actual size

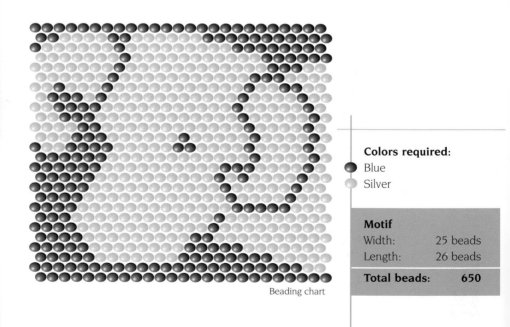

Beading chart

Colors required:
- Blue
- Silver

Motif	
Width:	25 beads
Length:	26 beads
Total beads:	**650**

Gemini

Symbolized by the
twins, those born
under this air sign
are said to be
curious, intellectual,
and mercurial.

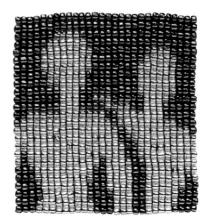

Actual
size

Beading chart

Colors required:
- Blue
- Silver

Motif	
Width:	28 beads
Length:	25 beads
Total beads:	**700**

Cancer

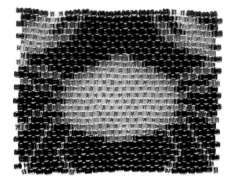

A water sign, and represented by the crab. Cancerians are said to be home-loving, warm, and friendly.

Actual size

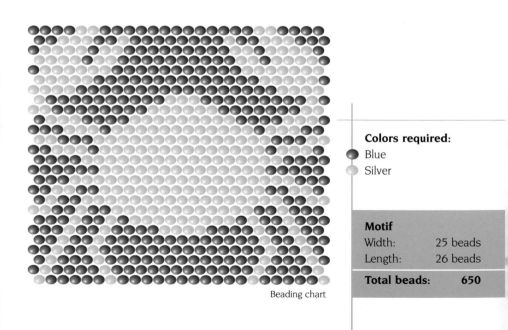

Beading chart

Colors required:
- Blue
- Silver

Motif	
Width:	25 beads
Length:	26 beads
Total beads:	**650**

Leo

Leo is represented by a lion, and is a fire sign. Leos are said to be bold, confident, and creative.

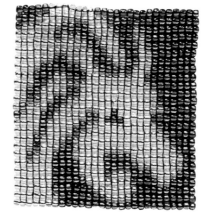

Actual size

Beading chart

Colors required:
● Blue
○ Silver

Motif	
Width:	28 beads
Length:	25 beads
Total beads:	**700**

Virgo

Virgo is an earth sign, and those born under it are said to be practical, quick-witted, and perfectionists.

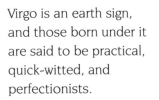

Actual size

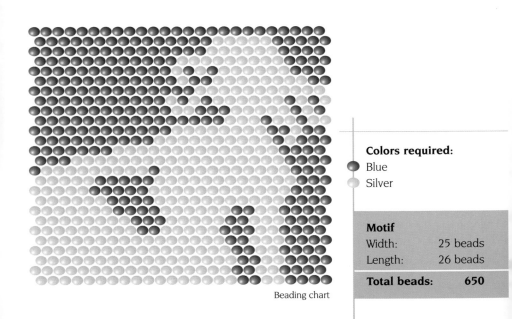

Beading chart

Colors required:
● Blue
○ Silver

Motif	
Width:	25 beads
Length:	26 beads
Total beads:	**650**

Libra

Represented by scales,
people born under this air
sign are said to be tactful,
decisive, and often creative.

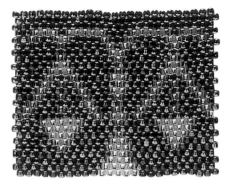

Actual
size

Beading chart

Colors required:

● Blue
○ Silver

Motif	
Width:	25 beads
Length:	26 beads
Total beads:	**650**

Scorpio

Scorpio is a water sign, and people born under this sign are said to be intense, secretive, and sensuous.

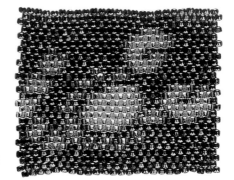

Actual size

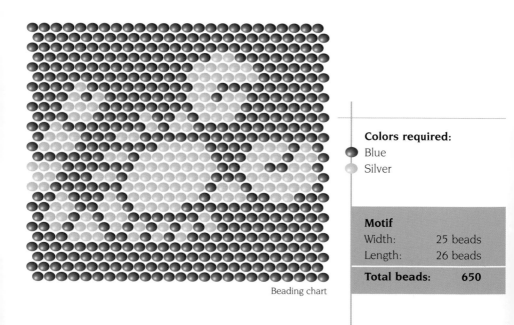

Beading chart

Colors required:
- Blue
- Silver

Motif	
Width:	25 beads
Length:	26 beads
Total beads:	**650**

Sagittarius

This fire sign is symbolized by the archer, and those born under Sagittarius are said to be optimistic, honest, and outgoing.

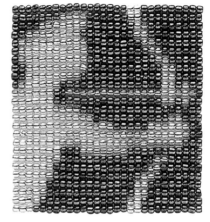

Actual
size

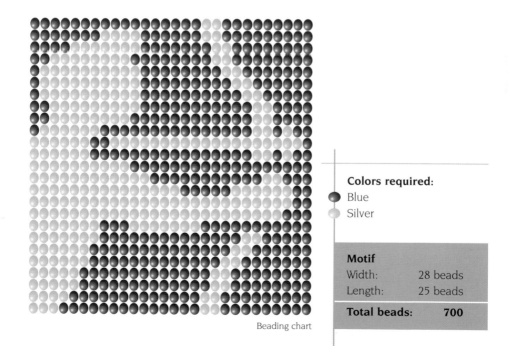

Beading chart

Colors required:
- Blue
- Silver

Motif	
Width:	28 beads
Length:	25 beads
Total beads:	**700**

Capricorn

Symbolized by the goat,
those born under this
earth sign are said to
be ambitious, loyal,
and industrious.

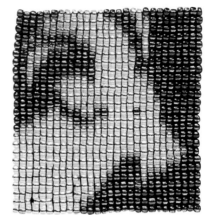

Actual
size

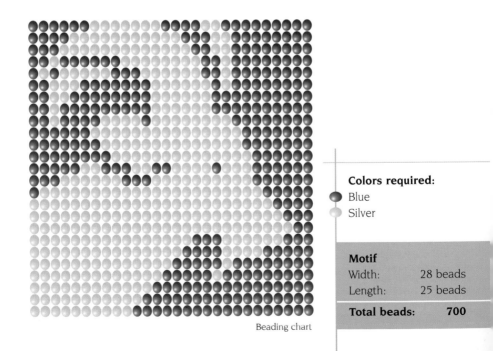

Beading chart

Colors required:

● Blue
○ Silver

Motif

Width:	28 beads
Length:	25 beads

Total beads:	**700**

Aquarius

Represented by the water-
bearer, Aquarius is an air
sign. Those born under this
sign are said to be mercurial,
intelligent, and idealistic.

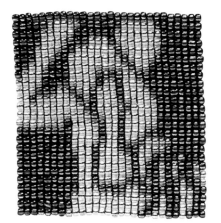

Actual
size

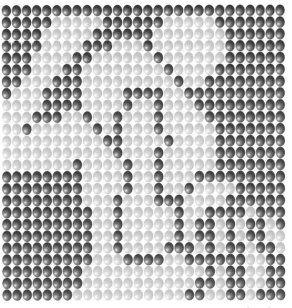

Beading chart

Colors required:
Blue
Silver

Motif	
Width:	28 beads
Length:	25 beads
Total beads:	**700**

Pisces

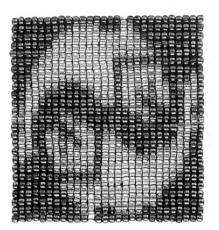

A water sign symbolized
by fish, those born under
Pisces are said to be
sensitive, adaptable,
and intuitive.

Actual
size

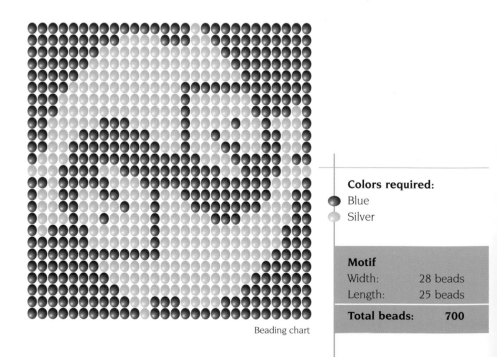

Beading chart

Colors required:

● Blue
○ Silver

Motif	
Width:	28 beads
Length:	25 beads
Total beads:	**700**

Zodiac Motifs

Here are the symbols of the zodiac in miniature. Why not weave one to put on a birthday card, or stitch all twelve in a row as a bracelet?

Aries

Taurus

Gemini

Cancer

Leo

Virgo

Libra

Scorpio

Sagittarius

Capricorn

Aquarius

Pisces

Colors required:
- Black
- Silver

Each motif	
Width:	10 beads
Length:	8 beads
Total beads:	**80**

LETTERS AND NUMBERS

Letters and numbers are always useful. A picture that includes the date is a lovely way to commemorate a special occasion, such as a wedding or christening.

Art Deco Alphabet

This alphabet has an Art Deco appearance, giving it a touch of class. You could weave an amulet bag with a friend's initial on one side and their favorite flower on the other, or stitch your name into a bracelet.

Each motif

Width:	25 beads
Length:	26 beads
Total beads:	**650**

Smaller than actual size

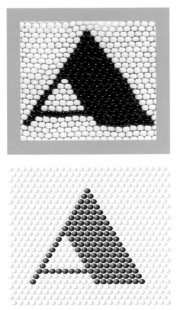

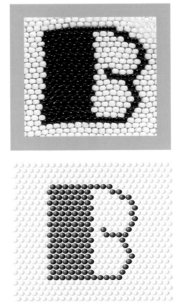

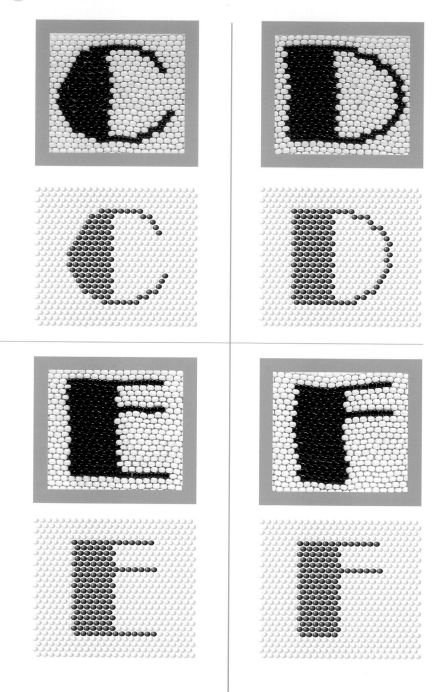

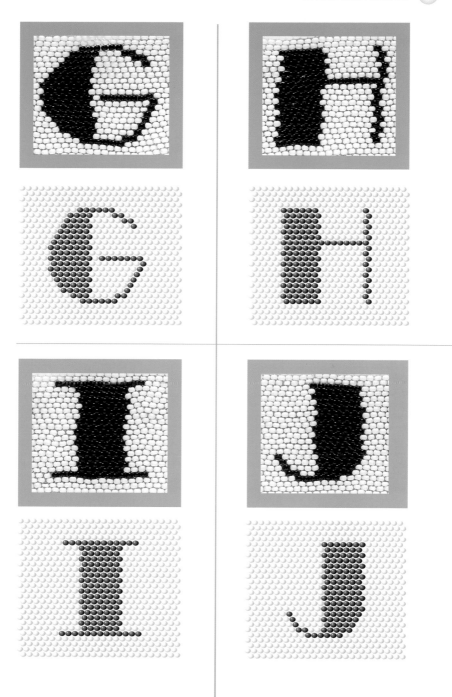

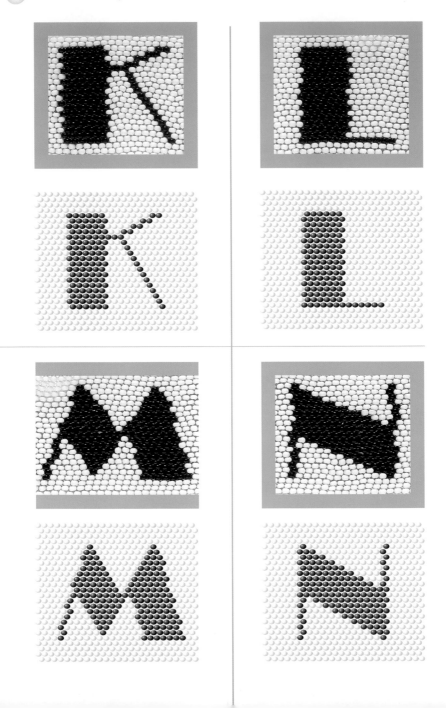

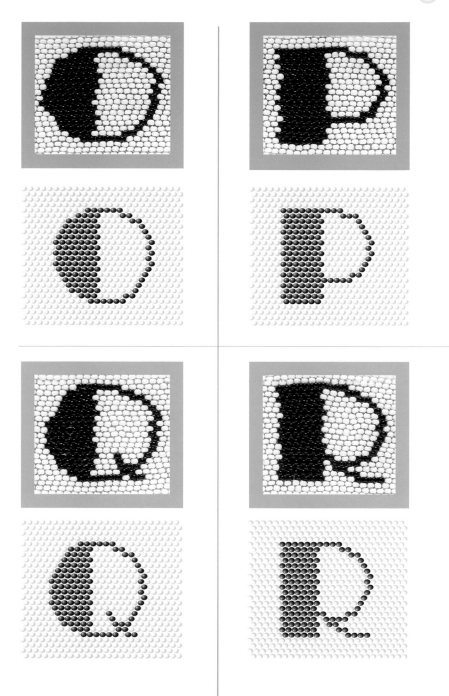

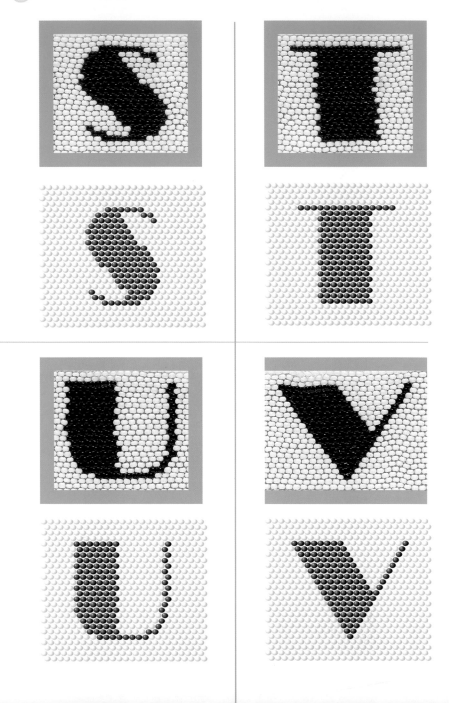

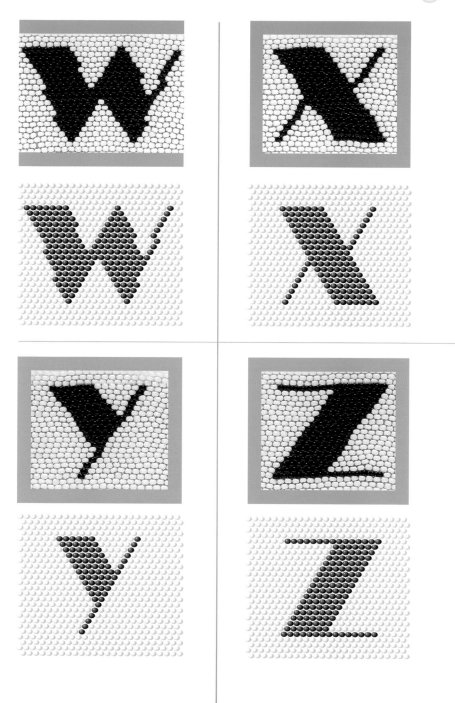

Art Deco Numbers

It's useful to know how to
weave numbers to feature
on greetings cards and gifts
for special occasions, such
as a 21st birthday or a 25th
wedding anniversary.

Each motif	
Width:	25 beads
Length:	26 beads
Total beads:	**650**

Smaller than actual size

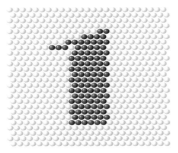

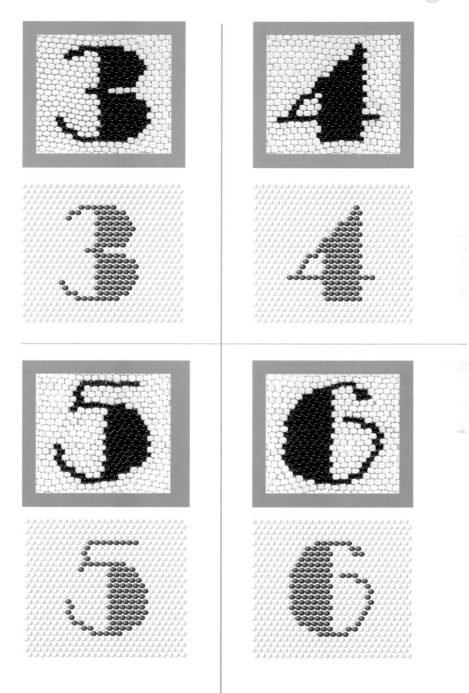

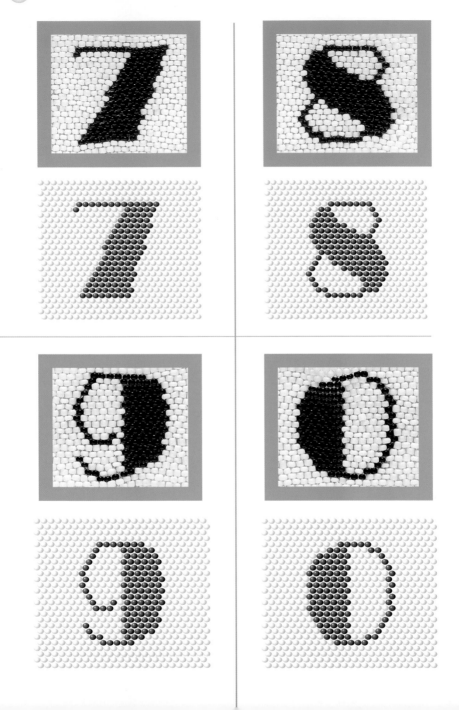

Small Alphabet & Numbers

This alphabet is designed to be woven as a strip, so you can use the motifs to spell out words or dates. Make sure you leave enough space between each letter or number—it might help to draw the design before you start weaving. This smaller design is ideal for bracelets and chokers, or if you want to add a name or date to another piece.

Each motif

Width:	variable
Length:	10 beads

Larger than actual size

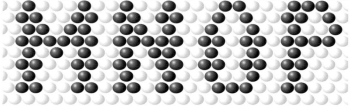

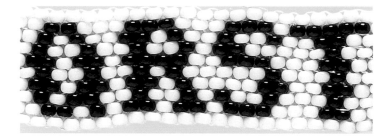

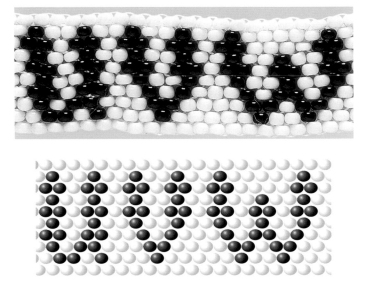

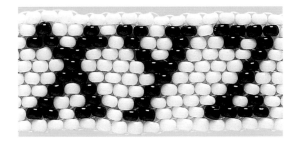

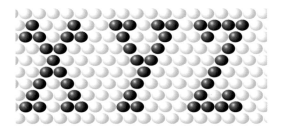

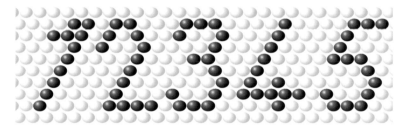

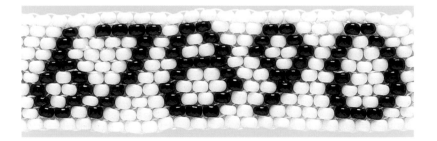

CELEBRATIONS

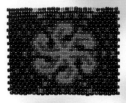

There is always something to celebrate, and in this range of patterns you will find inspiration for a gift or memento to commemorate the occasion. Alternatively, bead a card, simply to let people know you are thinking of them.

Champagne

When congratulations
are in order, a glass of
sparkling champagne
is always welcome.

Actual
size

Beading chart

Colors required:
- Black
- Blue
- Gray
- White
- Dark green
- Gold
- Champagne

Motif	
Width:	28 beads
Length:	25 beads
Total beads:	**700**

Birthday Cake

A chocolate and cream birthday cake with lots of pink frosting, topped with a candle and with confetti scattered all around. Perfect for any birthday celebration.

Actual size

Beading chart

Colors required:
- Dark pink
- Light pink
- Pale blue
- Green
- Brown
- Cream
- Yellow
- White

Motif

Width:	25 beads
Length:	26 beads
Total beads:	**650**

Balloons

Every celebration party needs plenty of balloons. You can easily change the colors on this pattern to match your own favorites.

Actual size

Beading chart

Colors required:

- Dark blue
- Light blue
- Red
- Black
- White
- Yellow

Motif

Width:	25 beads
Length:	26 beads
Total beads:	**650**

Graduation

Mark that special day of achievement with this pattern of an academic's mortar board and scroll.

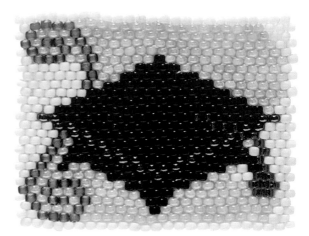

Larger than actual size

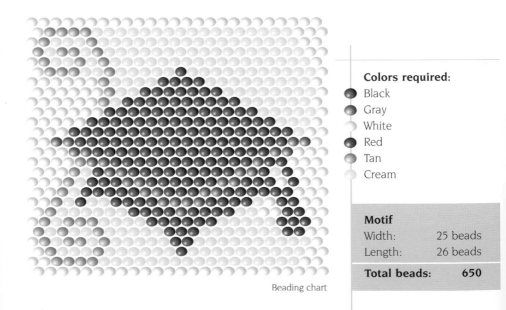

Beading chart

Colors required:
- Black
- Gray
- White
- Red
- Tan
- Cream

Motif	
Width:	25 beads
Length:	26 beads
Total beads:	**650**

Key to the Door

This key would work well for a 21st birthday, or if you prefer, change the number to suit a different "coming of age" celebration.

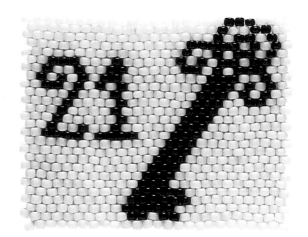

Larger than actual size

Beading chart

Colors required:
- Black
- White

Motif	
Width:	25 beads
Length:	26 beads
Total beads:	**650**

Christmas Tree

A Christmas tree decorated for the holiday season. Use silver-lined beads for the baubles and dark green beads for the tree for maximum sparkle.

Actual size

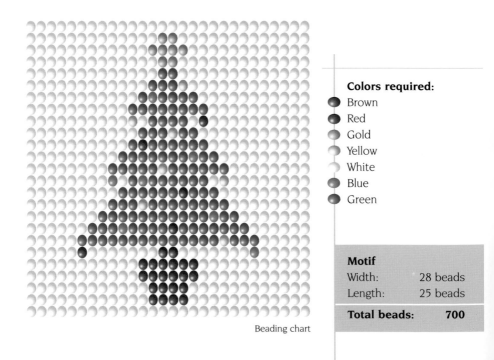

Colors required:
- Brown
- Red
- Gold
- Yellow
- White
- Blue
- Green

Motif	
Width:	28 beads
Length:	25 beads
Total beads:	**700**

Beading chart

Bauble

A shiny glass bauble ready
to decorate the Christmas
tree, or to adorn a festive
greeting card.

Actual
size

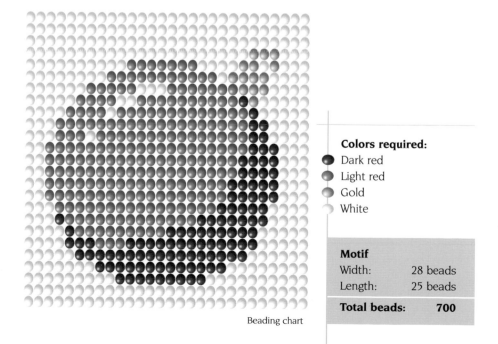

Colors required:
- Dark red
- Light red
- Gold
- White

Motif	
Width:	28 beads
Length:	25 beads
Total beads:	**700**

Beading chart

Christmas Pudding

A plump Christmas
pudding topped
with brandy sauce
and a festive sprig
of holly.

Larger than
actual size

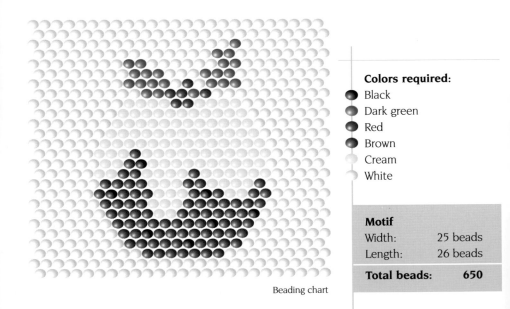

Beading chart

Colors required:
- Black
- Dark green
- Red
- Brown
- Cream
- White

Motif	
Width:	25 beads
Length:	26 beads
Total beads:	**650**

Father Christmas

The traditional story of Father Christmas brings excitement to children around the world during the holiday season.

Larger than actual size

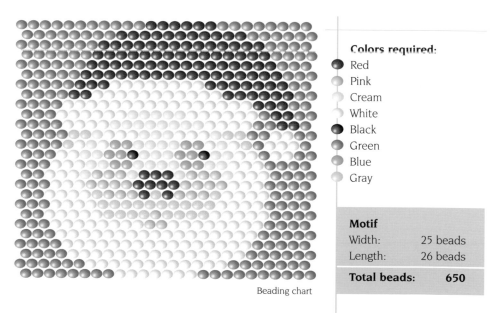

Beading chart

Colors required:

- Red
- Pink
- Cream
- White
- Black
- Green
- Blue
- Gray

Motif	
Width:	25 beads
Length:	26 beads
Total beads:	**650**

Robin

A festive robin perched on a bough of holly. This would be a good design for a Christmas greeting card.

Actual size

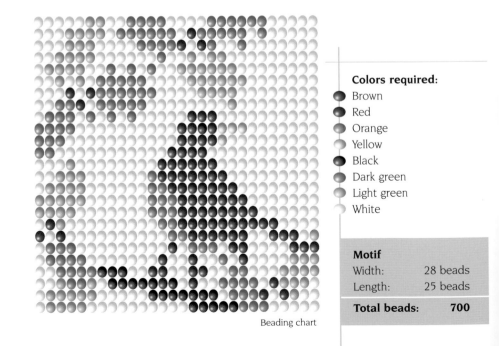

Beading chart

Colors required:
- Brown
- Red
- Orange
- Yellow
- Black
- Dark green
- Light green
- White

Motif	
Width:	28 beads
Length:	25 beads
Total beads:	**700**

New Home

A simple pattern—rather like a child's drawing of a house—that's ideal for a housewarming gift.

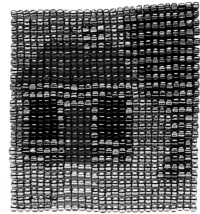

Actual size

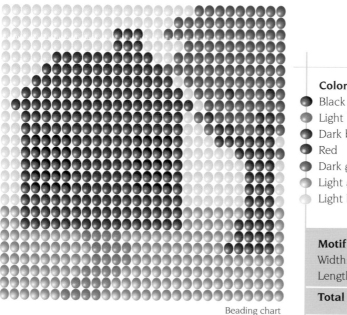

Beading chart

Colors required:

- Black
- Light brown
- Dark brown
- Red
- Dark green
- Light green
- Light blue

Motif	
Width:	28 beads
Length:	25 beads
Total beads:	**700**

Heart Wreath

A delicate design featuring a heart-shaped wreath entwined with flowers, perfect for the one you love on Valentine's Day.

Actual size

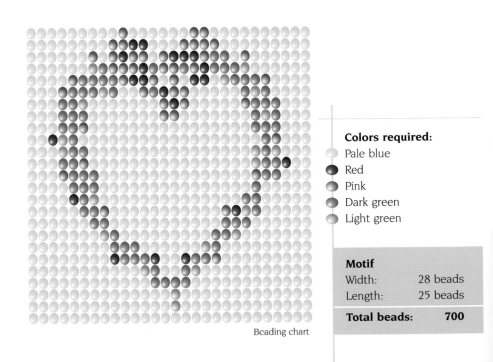

Beading chart

Colors required:
- Pale blue
- Red
- Pink
- Dark green
- Light green

Motif

Width:	28 beads
Length:	25 beads

Total beads:	**700**

Wedding Cake

A traditional, three-tiered wedding
cake decorated with bands of blue
ribbon and flowers and leaves.

Actual
size

Beading chart

Colors required:
Pink
White
Gray
Very light blue
Light blue
Green

Motif	
Width:	28 beads
Length:	25 beads
Total beads:	**700**

Horseshoe

The horseshoe is often seen at weddings, to bring good luck to the newly-wed couple. This design is ideal for a greeting card.

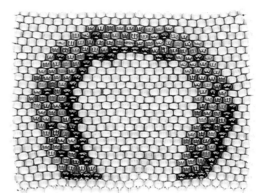

Larger than actual size

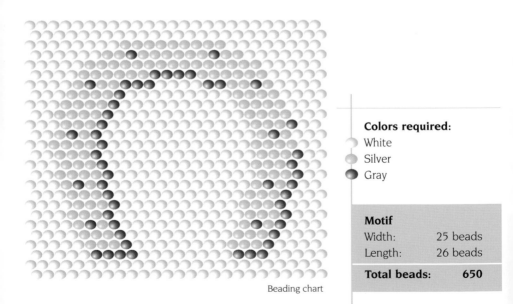

Beading chart

Colors required:
- White
- Silver
- Gray

Motif	
Width:	25 beads
Length:	26 beads
Total beads:	**650**

Rattle

A baby's rattle,
beaded in soft
pastel colors, is the
perfect design to
greet a new arrival.

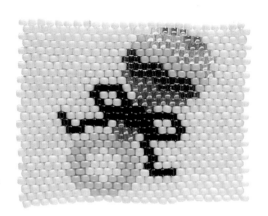

Larger than
actual size

Beading chart

Colors required:
- Pink
- Green
- Yellow
- Dark blue
- Light blue
- White

Motif	
Width:	25 beads
Length:	26 beads
Total beads:	**650**

Teddy Bear

This cute teddy bear
sporting a large bow
tie would be ideal for
a get well message,
for welcoming a new
baby, or celebrating
a child's birthday.

Actual
size

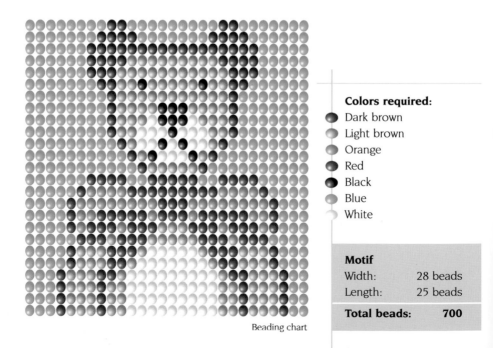

Beading chart

Colors required:
- Dark brown
- Light brown
- Orange
- Red
- Black
- Blue
- White

Motif	
Width:	28 beads
Length:	25 beads
Total beads:	**700**

Trophy

A silver trophy to celebrate
any great occasion, but
particularly suitable for
a sporting triumph.

Actual
size

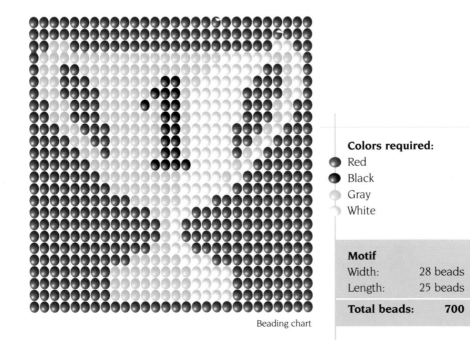

Beading chart

Colors required:

- Red
- Black
- Gray
- White

Motif	
Width:	28 beads
Length:	25 beads
Total beads:	**700**

Rocket

A rocket exploding sparks across an inky blue sky. To make this firework stand out, use silver-lined beads against a black background.

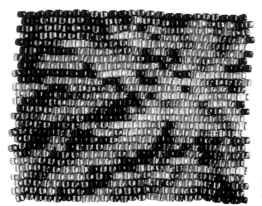

Larger than actual size

Beading chart

Colors required:

- Black
- Dark blue
- Light blue
- White

Motif	
Width:	25 beads
Length:	26 beads
Total beads:	**650**

Catherine Wheel

A Catherine wheel spinning against the night sky. This pattern would be great for an amulet bag. To make the firework sparkle, use silver-lined beads against a plain black background.

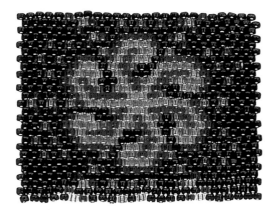

Larger than actual size

Beading chart

Colors required:
- Black
- Red
- Orange
- Yellow

Motif

Width:	25 beads
Length:	26 beads
Total beads:	**650**

Pumpkin

This cheerful pumpkin beaded in bright orange is perfect for celebrating either Hallowe'en or Thanksgiving.

Actual size

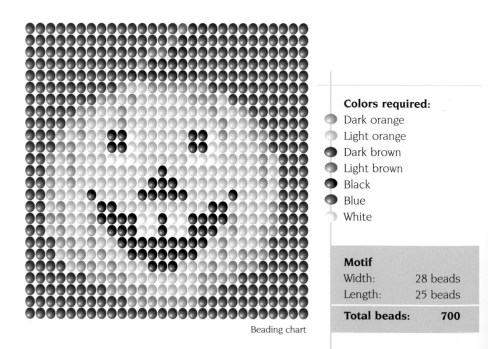

Beading chart

Colors required:

- Dark orange
- Light orange
- Dark brown
- Light brown
- Black
- Blue
- White

Motif	
Width:	28 beads
Length:	25 beads
Total beads:	**700**

Shamrock

The four-leaved clover or shamrock is a traditional symbol of good luck. Use two shades of green to emphasize the shape of the leaves.

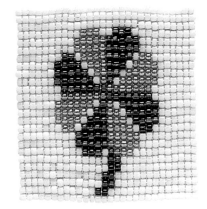

Actual
size

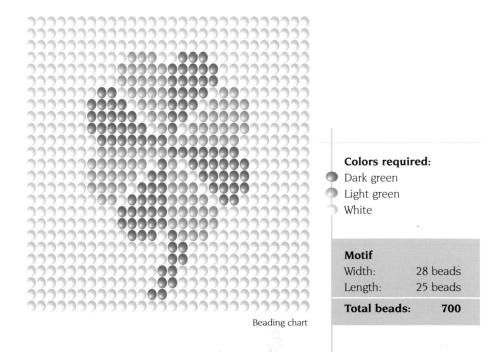

Beading chart

Colors required:
- Dark green
- Light green
- White

Motif	
Width:	28 beads
Length:	25 beads
Total beads:	**700**

Celebration Borders

A selection of borders for many occasions. You could use the ribbon or rainbow for birthdays, the trees for Christmas, and the hearts for Valentine's Day. To extend these patterns to the length you need, simply start at the beginning each time you reach the end of the pattern. You can then use these to make bracelets, chokers, and napkin rings.

Colors required:
Ribbon
Red
Dark blue
Light blue

Beading chart

Larger than actual size

Larger than actual size

Beading chart

Colors required:
Christmas trees
Dark green
Dark brown
White
Dark blue

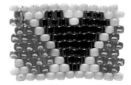

Larger than actual size

All motifs
Width: variable
Length: 10 beads

Colors required:
Hearts
Pink
White
Red

Beading chart

Beading chart

Colors required:
Rainbow and ark
Dark blue
Light blue
Red
White
Light brown
Dark brown
Light green
Black
Yellow
Orange

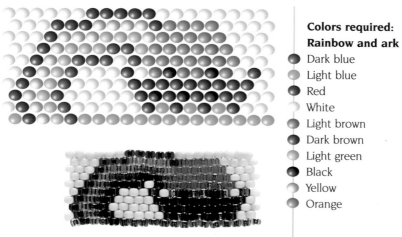

Larger than actual size

Small Celebrations

These small patterns are fun to use on their own to decorate cards or pictures, or why not link them together, with a couple of rows of beads in another color to make a bracelet?

All motifs actual size

Beading charts

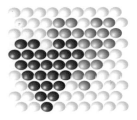 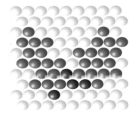 

Colors required:
Twin hearts
● Red
● Pink
○ White

Colors required:
Holly
● Dark green
● Red
○ White

Colors required:
Star
● Dark blue
○ White
● Gold

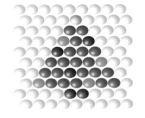

Colors required:
Christmas tree
● Dark green   ● Red
● Light blue   ○ White
○ Yellow   ● Brown

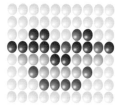 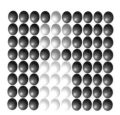 

All motifs actual size

Beading charts

 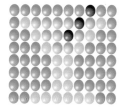

Colors required:
Kiss
- Cream
- Dark red
- Red
- Light red
- Pink

Colors required:
Cocktail
- Light blue
- Pink
- Black
- Gray

Colors required:
Candle
- Dark blue
- White
- Yellow
- Orange

All motifs
Width: 10 beads
Length: variable

Colors required:
Cracker
- Red
- Dark blue
- White

FINISHING OFF

Now that you have beaded a
selection of designs, you will
want to know how to use them.
This chapter explains how to
frame them as pictures, use
them as tiebacks and napkin
rings, create greeting cards,
turn them into amulet
bags, or add clasps
to make jewelry.

Fringes add a feeling of movement and richness to a piece of beadwork, and are very simple to add. You may wish to include some embellishment beads in a fringe.

Adding a fringe to peyote or brick stitch

1 Fasten on a new piece of thread, and weave through the work so it exits from a bottom corner bead.

2 Pick up all the beads for one strand of fringe, and slide them down the thread. Pass back through all the fringe beads except for the last bead added.

3 Holding onto the last bead on the length of the fringe, pull the thread gently to tighten so that very little is showing, but don't pull it too tight or the fringe will become stiff and won't drape properly.

4 Pass back up through the bottom corner bead of the piece of beadwork, and down through the next bead along. Add the next strand in the same way.

5 Continue until you've added the entire fringe. Fasten off as usual.

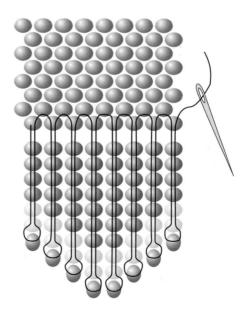

Adding a fringe to square stitch

1 Fasten on a new piece of thread and weave it through the work until you reach the bottom row. Pass through one of the bottom corner beads so you enter the bead on the outside edge of the beadwork.

2 Follow steps 2 and 3 of adding fringe to peyote or brick stitch (see page 245).

3 Pass through the bottom corner bead, entering from the outside edge as before, and through the next bead along the bottom row. Add the next strand of fringe in the same way.

4 Continue until you have added the entire fringe. Fasten off as usual.

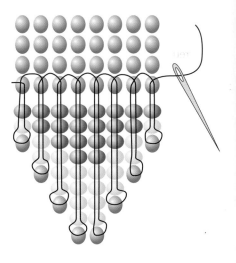

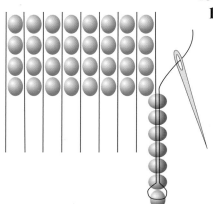

Adding a fringe to loom work

1 Thread the needle onto one of the warp threads coming out of the bottom row.

2 Follow steps 2 and 3 of adding fringe to peyote or brick stitch (see page 245).

3 Weave the end of the thread into the work as normal.

4 Repeat these steps for each warp thread.

Barrettes

Adorn your hair with
your favorite pieces
of beadwork.

1 The beadwork needs to be
a thin strip, due to the shape of the
barrette, so use either a border pattern
or one of the small motifs.

2 Weave a strip of beadwork ½–¾in
(1–2cm) longer than the barrette back.

3 Attach barrette back to the center
of the beadwork using strong glue.

4 Fold the ends of the beadwork over
the barrette back and glue in place. You
may need to tape them in position
until the glue has set.

Bracelets
and chokers

Why not make bracelets and chokers
to match all your favorite outfits, or as
presents? Choose one of the patterns
that repeat, or select small motif(s) and
repeat them.

1 Weave a piece of beadwork long
enough to fit around your wrist or neck
once the clasp is added.

2 Weave the thread through the
beadwork so it exits in the middle
of one side, where you wish to
add a clasp.

3 Pick up four beads, one half of
the clasp, and another four beads.
Weave into the beadwork in a loop
so the thread exits in the middle
of the side again.

4 Pass back through the beads and
the clasp to reinforce it. Fasten off the
thread as usual. Attach the other half
of the clasp in the same way.

Brooches

Beadwork can be made into stunning brooches, especially if a fringe is added. Using a piece of cardboard will stiffen the beadwork, making it easier to wear as a brooch.

1 Cut a piece of stiff cardboard about ¼in (5mm) smaller than the piece of beadwork, and glue a brooch back to the center of the cardboard.

2 Cut a piece of ultrasuede or suedette about ½in (1cm) larger than the cardboard. Put this over the cardboard, ensuring the cardboard is in the center of the fabric. Mark the raised ends of the brooch back lightly on the fabric. Use these marks to cut two small slits.

3 Cover the cardboard on the side with the brooch back with a thin layer of glue. Open the brooch back and slip on the fabric, smoothing it in place.

4 Close the brooch back and turn the cardboard over. Fold the edges of the fabric over the cardboard, and glue down. Cut notches in the corners of the fabric so the fabric folds in neatly.

5 Cover this side of the cardboard and fabric with a thin layer of glue, and stick on the piece of beadwork.

Keyrings

Why not use pieces of beadwork to decorate your keys. Attach keyrings to a piece of beadwork in the same way as you attach a clasp for a choker or bracelet.

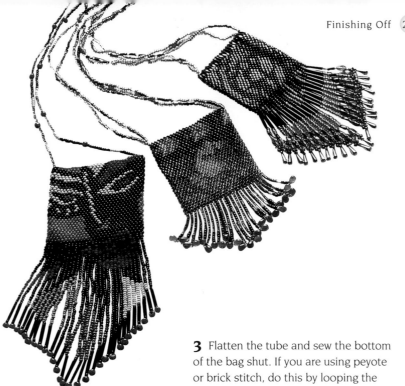

Amulet bags

Amulet bags are a traditional form of beadwork and a great way to display your work. Or if you prefer not to wear them, why not hang them on the wall like the artwork that they are?

1 Choose your pattern and weave a piece of beadwork twice as wide as the original. You can do this by repeating the same pattern, choosing another pattern to weave for the back of the bag, or weave an unpatterned colored section to the right size.

2 Roll this piece into a tube, and join the two sides together.

3 Flatten the tube and sew the bottom of the bag shut. If you are using peyote or brick stitch, do this by looping the thread through the loops of thread between the beads. For square stitch or loom work, close the bottom of the bag in the same way as joining a section of brick stitch (see page 29).

4 If you wish, add a fringe across the bottom of the bag (see pages 245–246).

5 Fasten on a new piece of thread and exit the bag at one of the top corners. String on beads to the length you need for the strap. Join the strap to the opposite top corner by weaving the thread into the beads in a loop so that the thread exits in the same place as it entered the top of the bag. Pass back through the strap to reinforce it. Fasten off as usual.

Greeting cards

Mark that special occasion with a handmade card. Look in your local craft store for blank cards and decorations among the card-making supplies. Decorate the card with attractive papers, and maybe some confetti, sequins, or a charm, making sure you leave enough room for your piece of beadwork. Then attach the beadwork using strong glue. For an extra touch, decorate the envelope with a few beads.

Pictures

If you want to hang your work on the wall, frame it first. Choose a simple frame that won't distract from your beadwork. It can look attractive to mount the beadwork on colored paper or fabric before framing. Use a mount of thick cardboard or mountboard in a co-ordinating color to surround the beadwork, and keep the glass in the frame away from the beadwork.

Curtain tiebacks

Add a bit of flair to your curtains with beaded curtain tiebacks.

1 Stitch a piece of beadwork about 20in (50cm) long.

2 Cut a piece of ultrasuede or suedette ½in (1cm) larger than the piece of beadwork all around. Fold over this hem all the way around and iron it flat.

3 Either stitch or glue the hem down, and then either stitch or glue the piece of beadwork to the fabric. Stitch a curtain ring to each end of the tieback.

Napkin rings

These are extremely simple to make but add an elegant touch to your dining table. Just stitch a piece of beadwork about 6in (15cm) long, and join the ends to make a tube. If you have particularly heavyweight napkins, you may need to make the beadwork a little longer. Why not make a set with each ring in a different color or pattern, perhaps with initials, so there is one for each person at your table? Make them to co-ordinate with your tablecloth or tableware, or give them as a house-warming present.

Resources

Austin Bead Society
P.O. Box 656
Austin, TX 78767-0656
Email: austinbeadsociety@yahoo.com
www.austinbeadsociety.org

Baltimore Bead Society
8510 High Ridge Road
Ellicott City, MD 21043
Email: baltbead@bcpl.net
www.baltobead.org

Bead Society of Greater Chicago
P.O. Box 8103
Wilmette, IL 60091-8103
www.bsgc.org

Bead Society of New Hampshire
P.O. Box 356
Atkinson, NH 03811
Email: beadsocietynh@yahoo.com
www.nebeads.com/BSNH

Cumberland Valley Bead Society
Box 41903
Nashville, TN 37204
Email: johnsoncaren@hotmail.com
www.cvbeads.net

Great Lakes Beadworkers Guild
P.O. Box 1639
Royal Oak, MI 48068-1639
www.greatlakesbeadworkersguild.org

International Society of Glass
Beadmakers
1120 Chester Avenue #470
Cleveland, OH 44114
www.isgb.org

Madison Bead Society
P.O. Box 620383
Middleton, WI 53562-0383
Email: madisonbeadsoc@hotmail.com
www.madisonbeadsociety.org

National Bead Society
3855 Lawrenceville Hwy.
Lawrenceville, GA 30044
Email: ibs@beadshows.com
http://nationalbeadsociety.com

Northwest Bead Society
P.M.B. 564
4603 N.E. University Village
Seattle, WA 98105
www.nwbeadsociety.org

Oklahoma Bead Society
Teresa Davis, Librarian
5144 S New Haven Ave.
Tulsa, OK 74135
Email: teresadavis50@hotmail.com
www.okbeadsociety.com

Portland Bead Society
P.O. Box 997
Portland, OR 97207-0997
www.beadport.com

Rocky Mountain Bead Society (RMBS)
P.O. Box 480721
Denver, CO 80248-0721
Email: rmbs@rockybeads.org
www.rockybeads.org

San Antonio Bead and Ornament Society
Email: sabostx@hotmail.com
www.homestead.com/sabostx/

South Jersey Bead Society
53 Sunset Drive
Voorhees, NJ 08043-4941
Email: prancingpixel@yahoo.com
www.southjerseybeadsociety.org

The Bead Museum
5754 W Glenn Drive
Glendale, AZ 85301
www.thebeadmuseum.com

The Bead Society of Greater New York
P.O. Box 6219
FDR Station
New York, NY 10150
Email: info@nybead.org
http://nybead.org

The Bead Society of Greater Washington
The Jenifer Building, Ground Floor
400 Seventh Street Northwest
Washington, DC 20004
Email: info@beadmuseumdc.org
www.bsgw.org

The Bead Society of Orange County
2002 N. Main Street
Santa Ana, CA 92706
www.beadsocietyoc.org

Upper Midwest Bead Society
3000 University Avenue SE, #5
Minneapolis, MN 55414
http://umbeads.tripod.com/

Wild West Bead Society
c/o Beads, Rocks and Knots
1730 W Randol Mill Rd. Suite 125
Arlington, TX 76012
Email: VickyBeads@dellepro.com
www.geocities.com/vickysbeads/index.html

Wyoming TumbleBeaders Bead Society
P.O. Box 1431
Cheyenne, WY 82003-1431
www.geocities.com/wyotumblebeaders/

Web sites

http://beadwork.about.com/
An American site with an active forum and a lot of links and articles.

http://members.cox.net/sdsantan/
beadfairies.html
Another resources site with quite a few links and tips.

http://www.interweave.com/bead/
The web site for the magazine *Beadwork*.

http://www.beadandbutton.com/
Bead and Button, another beading magazine.

http://www.beadingtimes.com/
An online beading magazine.

Index

Acknowledgments

Author's Acknowledgments

Bead Fairies

With many thanks to the following beaders (from BritishBeaders: http://groups.yahoo.com/group/britishbeaders) who helped to stitch the designs:
Amanda Appleton
Ugugunega
Avril Heron
Jean Power (www.beadelicious.com)
Kate George
(http://homepage.ntlworld.com/kate.george)
Heather Fenn-Edwards
(www.MooncatcherDesigns.co.uk)
Siân Mayer
Denise Chapman
Anne-Claire Lubek
Carole Tucker
Ms. Umbreen Hafeez
Susan Frith
Jacqueline Smith
Lesley Nutbeam
Lorraine Fryer
Maria Crouchley

Designs

Maria Crouchley (www.bearhugs.co.uk)
Claire Crouchley (www.bearlybeaded.co.uk)

Bead Supplier

The author and publishers would also like to thank GJ Beads for kindly supplying all the beads for the designs featured in this book. See their website for full details of the range of beads and equipment they can supply.

GJ Beads
Court Arcade
The Wharf
St Ives
Cornwall TR26 1LG
Tel: 01736 793886
www.gjbeads.co.uk